HAWKEYE COMMUNITY COLLEGE
3 7944 1017 9518 2

D0140812

WITHDRAWN

AD CRIT- IQUE

659.1 T125
Tag, Nancy R
Ad critique : how to
deconstruct ads in order to
build better advertising
ocm730403667

659.1
T125

AD CRIT- IQUE

HOW TO DECONSTRUCT ADS IN ORDER TO BUILD BETTER ADVERTISING

Nancy R. Tag
The City College of New York

$SAGE

Los Angeles | London | New Delhi
Singapore | Washington DC

Los Angeles | London | New Delhi
Singapore | Washington DC

FOR INFORMATION:

SAGE Publications, Inc.
2455 Teller Road
Thousand Oaks, California 91320
E-mail: order@sagepub.com

SAGE Publications Ltd.
1 Oliver's Yard
55 City Road
London, EC1Y 1SP
United Kingdom

SAGE Publications India Pvt. Ltd.
B 1/I 1 Mohan Cooperative Industrial Area
Mathura Road, New Delhi 110 044
India

SAGE Publications Asia-Pacific Pte. Ltd.
33 Pekin Street #02–01
Far East Square
Singapore 048763

Acquisitions Editor: Matthew Byrnie
Editorial Assistant: Elizabeth Borders
Production Editor: Astrid Virding
Copy Editor: Gillian Dickens
Typesetter: Hurix Systems Pvt. Ltd.
Proofreader: Dennis W. Webb
Indexer: Molly Hall
Cover Designer: Rose Storey
Marketing Manager: Liz Thornton
Permissions Editor: Karen Ehrmann

Copyright © 2012 by SAGE Publications, Inc.

All rights reserved. No part of this book may be reproduced or utilized in any form or by any means, electronic or mechanical, including photocopying, recording, or by any information storage and retrieval system, without permission in writing from the publisher.

Printed in the United States of America

Library of Congress Cataloging-in-Publication Data

Tag, Nancy R.
Ad critique : how to deconstruct ads in order to build better advertising / Nancy R. Tag.

p. cm.
Includes bibliographical references and index.

ISBN 978-1-4129-8053-1 (pbk.)

1. Advertising. 2. Advertising—Evaluation. 3. Criticism.
I. Title.

HF5823.T155 2012

659.1—dc23

2011032015

This book is printed on acid-free paper.

11 12 13 14 15 10 9 8 7 6 5 4 3 2 1

Contents

Acknowledgments

So many people have helped bring this book to life. First, I must thank Todd Armstrong at SAGE Publications who saw the promise and made it happen. My new editorial and production staff at Sage has been a dream team. Thanks to my editor, Matt Byrnie, for picking up the ball and running with it. Elizabeth Borders has been the consummate "go to" person. Thanks also to the steady contributions of Nathan Davidson and Aja Baker as well as the eagle-eye of Gillian Dickens and the production editing skills of Astrid Virding.

A special thanks to my reviewers, Maureen McAllister (The New School for General Studies; Parsons The New School for Design) and Karen Mallia (University of South Carolina), who were both great champions of the material, and Sheri J. Broyles (University of North Texas), Tim Hendrick (San Jose State University), Karie Hollerbach (Southeast Missouri State University), Robin Landa (Kean University), Timothy P. Meyer (University of Wisconsin–Green Bay), and Olaf H. Werder (New Mexico), who offered up meaningful crits of their own—your suggestions have made this a better book. To Janet Dracksdorf: thanks for reading the fine print. *Ad Critique* would not have been possible without years of collaboration with clients, Account Managers, and other colleagues in the ad industry. I'm lucky to have learned so much from my many creative partners—the best Art Directors in the business (Josh, Katherine, John, and Nick). This book is also the result of my many years in the classroom at City College, Parsons School of Design, and the Fashion Institute of Technology. I've learned so much from you all. My students rock. An extra special thanks to Lynn Appelbaum and the faculty at CCNY, including Ed Keller, Lynne Scott Jackson, and Andrea Weiss. I'm grateful to Natalie Henry, my student assistant. Big thanks to Gerardo Blumenkrantz—stellar enthusiast and awesome illustrator. The "couldn't have done it without you" award goes to Ann, Lisa, and Sarah (GGW) with hugs. As always, my lifelong sounding board deserves all my loving gratitude: Speedo, Popeye, and the amazing Beev.

Finally, this is for the boys: Nick, Nicky, and Jack. It's nothing without you.

Introduction

Nobody reads introductions.

So let's make this short and sweet. You need this book. If you've picked it up and cracked the spine, you're interested enough in advertising to need the skills that this book teaches. For students and professionals, business-minded types and creative folks, nothing is more valuable to the creation of great advertising than the ability to talk about it meaningfully. This skill is called critique. Without it, you have to rely on others to tell you what's right and what's wrong. With it, you can help determine your own destiny. Almost scary, eh? Well, yeah. That's because no one really teaches this sort of thing. This book does. If courage were a language, it would be called critique. And it's time that everyone who has a stake in advertising learned it.

Here's an overused proverb. It may seem stale, but I like it. It works. And if it works, it's as good as fresh.

> *Give a man a fish, feed him for a day. Teach a man to fish, feed him for a lifetime.*

Let me explain its relevance. There are many opportunities to see great works of advertising—award shows, annuals, textbooks. There are many, many more opportunities to see truly horrific works of advertising—magazines, television, the Internet. In other words: everywhere you look. 24/7. The thing is, few of us are ever taught how to distinguish between the two, especially *in process,* which is the best time to actually affect its outcome.

Ad Critique is less concerned about defining what's effective advertising and what isn't. The main thing here is to teach you how to look at an ad, talk about it meaningfully, and help decipher its value at any given moment in the process. With this skill, you're less likely to respond to the work in front of you by saying, "I wish this were as good as the 'got milk?' campaign." Instead, you're more likely to have a meaningful conversation about the work. This is not only more constructive, but it also helps you achieve your own particular advertising needs. In other words, this book isn't about fish. It's about fishing. It's about learning a skill.

In the digital age where Marshal McLuhan's adage "the medium is the message" is our reality on steroids, this skill should come as great comfort. New media is always on our minds these days, so anything that helps us navigate the waters is a relief. However—and this is important—in order to learn critique skills, you're going to have to slow down a bit and understand how advertising creativity works. And the best way to do that is by focusing on print ads. That's not to be "old school." Or to suggest some advertising hierarchy. No, the reason for this emphasis on print is simply because it's the best teaching tool for learning critique skills. I'll tell you why later. After all, this is just the introduction (and no one reads introductions). Once you get the basic skills down, they can be applied more specifically to other media. We'll definitely touch upon how to do that; it's just not the point of the book. Yes. Yes. We must all fully appreciate the ever-changing media landscape as it morphs into something new and newer somewhere, somehow at this very instant! But the speed of obsolescence is a lesson in and of itself: Rather than drown in the particulars, it's important to acquire the sort of critical thinking that will allow us to cope with whatever comes our way.

No one could argue with the importance of critical thinking. It's the main goal of an educated society. Correct? But what you may not realize is that critique is the way that critical thinking is put into words. Critical thinking is what goes on in your brain. Critique is what comes out of your mouth. Critical thinking is private. Critique is public; it's partly how your critical thinking is judged. Aren't you glad you picked up this book?

Ad Critique will also dedicate a significant portion of this book to showing you how to put critique into action—in meetings, through dialogue, with sensitivity to each participant in the process and his or her role in it. Critique can't happen in a vacuum; indeed, it's a critical element to the collaborative process that's the hallmark of the advertising industry (or so I hear). The actual practice of critique is what transforms this nice little book into a tool in your communication arsenal. Hopefully, *Ad Critique* will teach you something that will make you more invested in the process and product of advertising. This should be true whether you're interested in being a successful Art Director or Copywriter, Account Executive, or brand manager. The larger goal is to create advertising that works—for everyone, including the consumer. And that just makes the world a better place to live in.

But let's not get too far ahead of ourselves. Let's become skillful. Let's get courageous.

Let's raise the bar. Let's begin. . . .

The Language of Critique

The Case for Critique

Why We Need Constructive Criticism to Make Great Ads

Befriending the Beast

As a professor of advertising, I begin each semester with the same statement: "Most advertising stinks." That doesn't mean there isn't plenty of terrific brand building, perception shaping, and hard-selling stuff on the airwaves and in the award books. But the vast majority of advertising is as invisible as wallpaper. Or as annoyingly offensive as gum on your shoe. At its worst, advertising can seem like a big, stinky beast that forces itself down our throats and leaves an ugly taste in our mouths. Consumers are inundated. Promoters become more beastly aggressive. We begin to lose sight of what we're looking at. This is bad. By definition, bad advertising is advertising that's ineffective. And ineffective means that it hasn't met its strategic objectives. By that measure, most would agree that there's more bad stuff out there than good. In other words, most advertising stinks.

This point must be made right upfront. Otherwise, you will be destined to mimic the advertising that we all experience in the real world and add to the pile of dreck that already exists. Of course, we're bound to do that to some degree anyway. Nobody's perfect. But if we can acknowledge this framework right upfront, it will begin to reshape our thinking.

Actually, most people are pretty relieved when an expert tells them that most advertising stinks because it pretty much confirms their own suspicions as everyday consumers. But it also begs the question: If bad advertising isn't effective, why is there so much of it? The answer is almost too obvious. The reason most advertising is bad is because it's really, really hard to create advertising that's good.

That's the simple truth. Good advertising is really hard to do. It relies on smart collaboration. Fresh strategic insight. And lots of creativity. Advertising can falter anywhere along the way. But the biggest wild card of all is the creativity part. It's unpredictable. Elusive. Difficult to evaluate. And yet creativity is so essential that campaigns can't survive without it. Without an ability to grab your attention and hold it, the message is just pen on paper. Therefore, creativity really *must* be a beast. Not a stinky beast, mind you. That would be bad. But a smart, feisty beast that roars.

This is what we call the "creative imperative." Creativity is not a discretionary component of advertising but part and parcel of it. But not everyone's ecstatic about this. Certainly the marketer's life would be so much easier if this weren't the case. This would make it easier to measure. Easier to predict. Easier to formulate. That's why business-minded people sometimes espouse reasons to dismiss the importance or even the need for creativity. Marketing textbooks warn management students to be wary of creativity. Many client meetings end with admonitions such as, "Don't let your creative people run amok!" Or, "We're not trying to win awards—we're here to sell the product!" Clients who say these sorts of things (you'll rarely hear these kinds of statements from Creative Directors) are usually less concerned about the particular weaknesses of any work than about a general fear of creativity itself. Wouldn't we all just be better off if we found some highly scientific, quantifiable way to execute advertising so all this "loosey goosey" stuff could just go away? Well, no. Anyone who truly feels this way has never understood the reasons behind the creative imperative. And unless you fully appreciate the creative imperative, you won't find the value in developing the skills of critique. So let's be unambiguous here. Advertising really does need creativity in order to work effectively. Bill Bernbach, a founder of the legendary ad agency Doyle Dane Bernbach, said it best himself:

> The truth isn't the truth
> until people believe you,
>
> and they can't believe you
> if they don't know what you're saying,
>
> and they can't know what you're saying
> if they don't listen to you,
>
> and they won't listen to you
> if you're not interesting,
>
> and you won't be interesting
> unless you say things
> imaginatively,
> originally,
> freshly.

This is irrefutable logic, don't you think? Bill Bernbach was a genius. An amazingly creative, astutely logical genius. As father of advertising's "Creative Revolution" back in the sixties, it's not surprising that he could make such an eloquent case for creativity; he came up from the creative side of the business, starting his career as a Copywriter. What's surprising is that the ironclad logic of this quote embodies another great truth about advertising: The best creative minds are astutely logical—which may seem counterintuitive to some people. Indeed, some think the hallmark of creativity is *illogic*. Not true, not in advertising. Logic may not always be immediately evident in the work, but ultimately there must be some explainable reason for why anything is verbalized, visualized, or experienced in advertising. Meaningful creativity should never be explained by "whatever." Or "it's subjective." That's a copout. Hearing such arbitrary comments over the years has justifiably filled business-minded people with fear whenever creative people enter the room. They fear that creativity has no boundaries. And worse: that creativity has no meaning. But when that's the case, the work shouldn't be defined as "creative"; it should be defined as bad. Creativity just tends to take the rap for it. That's not only unfair but also a huge reason for the vast management/ creative divide.

So now we've got two main, truly fundamental points on the table. First: In advertising, creativity is imperative. Second: Being creative doesn't equal total freedom. Art Directors are not fine artists designing ads to express their inner angst. Copywriters are not toiling away to create the next great American novel. They should be a disciplined lot beholden to their client, the consumer, and their fresh imaginations—all at the same time. This means that both sides of the divide need to recalibrate their expectations to some extent. Businesspeople need to embrace creativity, not dismiss it. Creative people need to know, quite definitively, that they can't be arbitrary; there is no "whatever" in advertising. Asking the two sides to shake hands and agree on these fundamental points may be asking too much, too early in the book. It would require an enormous leap of faith. And why leap when the chasm still seems so wide? However, if both sides had a shared skill—or shared language—perhaps they could more easily reach their shared goals. Perhaps they could bridge the chasm. Then these fundamental points could not only be agreed upon but also truly believed in.

That skill is called critique.

What Exactly Is Critique?

Critique is basically a discussion-based evaluation of work. Most people, however, don't know exactly what that means. Unless you've done a stint in art college where "crits" are a fundamental element of your studio classes, you may have never experienced a facilitated or formal critique in school. Instead, when most students write a term paper, it's submitted directly to the teacher. That's a private act. And the feedback is more or less private through comments directly on the work, in the form of an evaluation rubric, or perhaps during a face-to-face meeting. Throughout your life as a student, it's rare to publicly discuss work in progress alongside its creator. The very thought of that can be mortifying, which this book will explore in great detail. But before tackling all that, the first hurdle to overcome is understanding what critique is. Nearly everyone gets it all wrong. Most think that critiquing is synonymous with being negative. And in the context of advertising, that sounds pretty appropriate. Everyone's a critic of advertising, right? That's very true. However, it's not what we're talking about here.

There's an enormous difference between "critique," in which one deconstructs an ad in order to understand it and construct something better, and "criticism," in which one complains about a commercial that's just interrupted his or her favorite TV show. Critiquing an ad or campaign concept is to talk about it meaningfully. Critique pulls the work apart, examines it, and determines if the elements make sense and if the whole comes together. It's about discussing whether strategic goals have been creatively and appropriately translated into engaging content. Critique enables constructive dialogue. It's key to the collaboration that defines the Art Director–Copywriter relationship. It's what happens when work is presented up and down the line within the Creative Department. It's what all those creative types do while they're drinking a beer after work and paying more attention to the ads on the TV set over the bartender's head. Critique is, quite simply, how work gets better.

Being good at critique doesn't just make the work better, it's also the reason why seasoned Art Directors and Copywriters have so much to say during creative presentations. They're used to talking about the work and what makes it effective. They may not even know that what they're doing is called critique, but it is. Indeed, it's so organic to them that they can't quite figure out why everyone else isn't as good at it. On the other side of the table, clients can be literally speechless after a creative presentation. They're not used to talking about creative work in a public forum. It's a skill that they've never really been taught, much less practiced. Imagine how disconcerting it must be for a high-level businessperson, who is used to being in command at business meetings, to suddenly lack fluency in a marketing matter of such importance. This is damaging not just to the psyche but also to the work. Without an ability to critique the work, there can be no real dialogue. It's as though both sides of the table are suddenly speaking different languages. The process becomes less productive. Relationships strain. The work suffers.

Anyone who's been to his or her share of presentations has seen this sort of management/creative interaction play out again and again. Creatives speak fluently about the work. Management folks look decidedly less comfortable. The industry has accepted these roles as a given without questioning whether anything could or even should be different. Where does this institutional mind-set begin? In the classroom. At any given moment, advertising professors across the country are showing samples of ad campaigns to their students and asking a simple question: "What makes this campaign work?" Chances are the response to that question will be pretty much the same: crickets. Or maybe students forget the academic setting and suddenly volunteer personal opinions—"Oh! I love that ad!" or "That's the worst!" The quality of the commentary usually degenerates from there as even the quietest students in the room start mimicking lines or goofy performances from their favorite commercials. From above the idle chatter, the professor tries to wrestle back control of the discussion by asking, "Why? Why do you think these commercials are effective?" Again, the response is crickets, only this time the silence is more deafening because the class had been so animated just seconds before. Frustrated, professors usually offer up their own critique or retreat to the safety of the textbook.

This scenario is common, yet it still leaves instructors peeved. In an age when so many students can recite the lines to their favorite commercials backwards and forwards, you'd assume that they're also gleaning some meaning from them—especially if they've chosen advertising as their college major. Yet when students are asked some pointed questions in an academic setting, silence prevails. What gives? Three things. First, like the future brand managers and account executives that many of them will become, they don't have a lot of critique experience to draw from. Second, no one has instructed them on the role or value of critique. And, finally, no one's actually taught them HOW to do it. As immersed as we all are in pop culture, the analysis of it is not a given. Indeed, because it's such a fun pastime to chat about advertising—it's the standard water-cooler conversation of our time—it's easy to confuse such chats with real critique. To complicate the issue, advertising seems averse to analysis; it's silly to think deeply about something as "silly" as advertising, even if the profession requires us to take it seriously. On top of all this, our culture has become so fast paced that we are less inclined to be reflective about *anything* of consequence—public policy, great literature, or art. Therefore, whether students are creative by nature or more business minded, instructors must truly force the issue. The ability to critique is not innate. It requires explicit instruction.

In addition to explicit instruction, the value of critique should be introduced at the very beginning of an advertising curriculum and then applied with each level of academic development. The critique muscle needs to be constantly exercised in order to get stronger. And it needs to be strong because critique gets harder as students move from theory to practice, from critiquing existing case studies to critiquing original work in progress. What exactly does that mean? Well, keep in mind that most people equate critiquing with being negative and mean. Most students hate to be mean—especially to their fellow students. So while most of us take a certain delight in anonymously bashing or yakking away about advertising that already exists on the airwaves or in print, once we start looking at work in progress in front of the person responsible for creating it, our impulse to bash or be loquacious transforms into a desire to be supportive or reticent. I can't tell you how many times I've listened to students totally decimate a long-running and effective advertising campaign yet conclusively say "I like it" to student work that has been given 3 minutes of thought on the subway ride up to school. Clearly, then, critique has progressive degrees of complexity and nuance. So if the theory of critique is not advanced with more involved and in-process forms of applied critique, the results will be . . . well, just academic.

Critique Is a Skill, Not a Talent . . .

Because creative professionals tend to be better at critique than business-minded professionals, we tend to think of critique as a talent and not a skill. But that just lets most people off the hook. If you're not born with it, why bother, right? However, critique is really a lot like presentation; it's an indispensable part of how we interact with the work and each other. Yet no one would dispute the need to teach presentation skills to students and professionals alike. The ad industry puts an enormous emphasis on presentation skills—with good reason. Even a great idea can die if it is not compellingly presented. That's why academic institutions teach presentation skills at all levels of their curricula. Once you've entered the field, presentation workshops top the list of professional development programs. But without complementing critique skills, a great presentation never reaches its full potential. Currently, most presentation training treats presentation as a static end point and one-way form of communication. That's wrong. The truth is, presentation is often part of a dynamic relationship with critique as its partner. Critique makes a presentation interactive and collaborative, making the audience participants as much as spectators.

Of course, many formal presentations only work well as one-way communication with a person at the podium and the audience at silent attention. But how many presentations do you go to in a day that really work like this? Most are touch points for collaboration and opportunities for dialogue. Without critique skills, we're not truly seizing these opportunities. The industry may give a lot of lip service to the importance of collaboration, but collaboration can't happen when the players don't all possess the same basic skill set. Being able to present the work is great. But without critique, it's just a performance and not part of a process. So we need to strengthen both sides of this dynamic relationship. And since it's commonly accepted that we can teach presentation skills, it's not a giant leap to believe that critique skills can be taught, too.

. . . So Let's Teach It

Now here's the good news. While the ability to critique is often the exclusive domain of the Creative Department, it's not an innate ability like creativity itself. The fact is, critique can be learned. Most business executives don't know this. Few business schools teach it. Experience fools many into believing that it's the native language of creative professionals. So let's be clear: It's not. Even Art Directors and Copywriters must be trained in it. Art Directors are immersed in it during design school where critique is a natural function of studio classes. Copywriters learn from being exposed to it in the Creative Department. Both Art Directors and writers hone their critique skills through the team partnership where ideas are constantly bounced around, discussed, dissected, rejected, and reinterpreted. It's no wonder that critique seems to come so easily to them. Of course, most business professionals will never need to develop a critique muscle as strong as their creative colleagues. But here's the really critical thing to know: We're all capable of it. With a little specialized training, business-minded professionals can not only become quite proficient at judging the creative product, but they can more meaningfully contribute to the process itself. The simple truth is that if every person responsible for the advertising were fluent in the language of critique, then everyone would have the tools to make the work better.

Whenever I teach a course in advertising, whether it's a creative course or a management course, I always emphasize three major aspects of the business: content generation (such as research, strategizing, conceptualizing, and execution), presentation, and critique. Students are familiar with the first two, but when I tell them that critique will be an integral part of the course, they usually freak out. Once, a student literally broke down and cried. "I can't do it. I hate to be mean to people!" she said. After I gave her a clear definition of what critique was and explained its value, she calmed down and asked the most perfect question of all: "Will you give us a language to work with?"

Little did she know that this is exactly at the core of critique. Acquiring that language and building a vocabulary requires a conscientious approach that needs to be explicitly taught. Then it needs to be put into practice, not just over the course of the semester but throughout any advertising curriculum. Only by actually participating in a facilitated critique week after week will students develop the skills essential to being a functioning advertising practitioner upon graduation. Otherwise, some will embark on their advertising careers, struggling in their jobs until they "get it"—eventually. Others will always struggle and remain mostly silent in meetings, delegating the lion's share of the discussion to others. Don't let that be you. Learn critique and take charge of your destiny.

Print: The Ground Zero of Critique

Why is *Ad Critique* so fixated on print? These days, there's no shortage of advertising vehicles out there. Television, digital, phone apps, in-game advertising, micro-blogging, product placement, experiential, viral, and on and on. Indeed, it's sort of like the Wild West out there. New media is being created, revised, and reworked and becoming obsolete all the time. Agencies, clients, and consumers struggle with all the changes, opportunities, and distractions. Our laws that regulate and codify these emerging forms of communication are lagging woefully behind. Even popular culture, which links identity to consumption, is on overload. While it would be totally inaccurate to call the traditional media of print and broadcast "antiquated," many would have no problem calling them "quaint."

So why the focus on print here? Not because of a personal bias, or because it's still one of the most effective means of mass communication—even though it is. The reason is because it's simply the best teaching tool for understanding the basic elements of advertising, the creative process, and the skills of critique. Here's why.

Print Is the Conceptual Bedrock of Advertising

Most Art Directors and Copywriters will tell you that they cut their creative teeth on print. To them, it's where visual and text come together to create communication magic. It's the blank page demanding a clever solution. It's where discipline is born. Essentially, if you want to understand the mechanics of creative thinking, studying print is like looking under the hood.

Print Is Touchable and Intimate

There should be a reason for selecting any particular communication vehicle. When it comes to print, there's nothing like the tactile feel of the paper, the reader's ability to control how close or far away his or her nose is from the paper, the opportunity to rip it out of a magazine and tape it to the wall. Readers feels like they "own" a print ad in a way they never feel with a TV commercial or a digital ad. As a student of critique, the closer you can get to your subject matter, the better.

Print Has the Power to Stop and Hold a Gaze

If a print ad is effective, the reader stops what he or she is doing and spends a little time with it. It's an interesting dynamic. On one hand, it reveals the strength of the ad. On the other, it gives the reader an amazing amount of control. Being able to evaluate this power is critical to appreciating the effectiveness of a strategic message and a creative concept.

Print Is Pure: It Doesn't Dance or Sing—Except in Your Mind

One of the reasons that print is such a great teaching tool is that it demands clarity of communication. There's little space and few dimensions to work with. This makes it a purer and simpler evaluative vehicle. As a student of critique, it's easier to understand the basic principles of effectiveness and the creative process that leads to it. It's easier to identify success or failure. Unlike other more collaborative media, such as television or digital, there are fewer distractions: no moving parts, no acting issues, no special effects, no jingles. When learning how to critique, print is like riding with training wheels. You need to get good at it before moving on to more acrobatic forms of advertising.

The Critique Paradox

The purpose of this book is to teach you how to become an expert at critique. But the more of an expert you become, the less able you are to respond to an ad like a typical consumer. Losing touch with the end user of your "product" is never a good thing. So in order for critique to be truly practical in the advertising world, you must be able to operate on a few contradictory levels at once. Welcome to the "critique paradox." As a professional, you need to take lots of time deconstructing the elements of an ad to determine if they make sense. Meetings about the meaning and effectiveness of an ad can take hours. The consumer, on the other hand, should get the gist of an ad's message within moments. This means that during a productive critique, you need to lavish time on the work while always being cognizant of the fact that the consumer should not.

As an expert in ad critique, you have a sharpened skill set and vocabulary that's very particular to marketing. While the general skills may be useful to you in other ways—being good at critique, for example, makes someone a great little league coach or parent—you're truly a specialist. The knowledge that you have about ads isn't shared by the general population. In a way, taking part in an ad critique is like speaking to ourselves. There's nothing wrong with that. Critique is crucial to the process. But the notion of "speaking to ourselves" can make people nervous because we'd never want our advertising to be like that. So we have to think like an expert and see like an amateur. And vice versa. Quite a paradox, eh?

As we learn critique, we must be mindful that there's no reason for consumers to be good at it. Being able to identify an ad's concept or target or strategy is critically important to us but not to our audience; indeed, saying that an ad's "strategy is showing" (meaning even the consumer can spot it) is considered an insult to the creative team. The better the ad, the less visible all the marketing mumbo jumbo is to the untrained eye. So if you see examples in the book and wonder if consumers would get any of this, you're right—they won't. This level of critique is really intended for professionals, even though the advertising itself is intended for the consumer. The trick here is to make friends with the paradox: Aspire to become as much of an omniscient expert as possible while still holding on to a piece of the unknowing consumer in your heart. It's no easy task but something else you'll need to master, or at least recognize, if you want to get the most out of critique.

Critique Basics

WHAT IS IT: A discussion-based evaluation of work, both in-process and post-process.

WHAT YOU GET OUT OF IT: Critique is a two-way street. It advances both the viewer's and the creator's understanding of the work. Which, in turn, advances the work.

Insight. The act of articulation is very powerful. It lays bare a work's strengths and weaknesses. Being able to put into words why a work is powerful confirms it power. On the other hand, being unable to articulate a work's worth can reveal its weaknesses. Discussion puts insights on the table for everyone to examine—sometimes in ways that had never been considered before. This leads to greater insight into both the work and process at hand.

Development. To some Art Directors and Copywriters, exposing work at certain points in the process is considered a necessary evil. Necessary because no advertising project exists in a vacuum. Evil because most of the comments made during these "check-ins" range from inane to insulting. However, productive critique is healthy to the development of a project. It's a time to share suggestions and refine the work. A meaningful critique moves the process forward in a constructive way, even if the work needs to be revised.

Access and collaboration. Anyone, from fellow creative colleagues to Account Managers, who knows how to offer valuable critique is not just tolerated but invited into the collaboration. Therefore, critique is the best way to ensure access not just to the product but to the process.

Communication. Critique gives the creative team a chance not only to talk about their thought processes but also to articulate how the work meets strategic objectives. In this way, critique bridges the chasm between strategic goals and artistic expression.

Persuasion. Advertising is about persuasion. Critique is an opportunity to convince an audience about the effectiveness of the work, thereby improving the skills of persuasion.

Thinking. Class critiques give students the opportunity to answer questions and respond to the comments in real time. This improves one's ability to look at creative work, to measure it against strategy, and to discuss it in an intelligent, organized, and constructive manner; in other words, you get better at critique. But that also leads to a greater understanding of people, process, and product. Such skills enable students to succeed not only as advertising professionals but in any field and any life endeavor.

Leadership. The person who can best articulate a true understanding of the work on the table takes on the leadership role in the room. People admire those who "get it," and the best way to prove that knowledge is through a meaningful critique.

HOW TO DO IT: Continue reading *Ad Critique*.

Further Reading

While this book focuses on the practical matter of critiquing ads *in process,* the study of ads with the intention of finding meaning has long been of scholarly interest.

For a greater understanding of how ads have been analyzed and decoded for various purposes and throughout history, read *ADText: Advertising Curriculum,* published by the Advertising Educational Foundation and distributed by Johns Hopkins University Press Project MUSE. The chapter on "The Interpretation of Advertising" by William M. O'Barr is particularly apt: http://muse.jhu.edu/journals/asr/v007/7.3unit09.html.

To fully appreciate the value of critique in advertising, it would helpful to consider the more general role of observation and thoughtful analysis in everyday life. *The Accidental Masterpiece* by Michael Kimmelman, chief art critic of *The New York Times,* is a reflection on seeing the world with a more observant eye and illustrates how critique enriches experience.

 Visit the student study site at www.sagepub.com/tagstudy for additional online resources including web links, video clips, and recommended readings to learn more about advertising and the creative process.

Critique Exercises

1. Go watch a recent blockbuster movie and write a 250-word critique of it. Read three movie reviews of the same movie, and list different aspects of the film that are critiqued and how deeply each aspect is discussed. Compare with your own critique.

2. In teams of two, interview each other on your qualifications to succeed in this class. Make a 2-minute presentation of the person you interviewed. Allow the class to critique your presentation, evaluating style, and content. Then let the person you interviewed critique you: How well did you capture this person?

3. Why is Bill Bernbach considered the father of the Creative Revolution? Look into that and present five ads created by Doyle Dane Bernbach in the sixties and explain why they represent a sea change in the industry.

CHAPTER 2

AdSpeak

The Vocabulary of Advertising

Every Language Needs a Vocabulary

During the early stages in the development of an ad campaign, the client and agency converse in the common language of marketing. Both parties are generally comfortable discussing things like macro-environmental trends, strategic brand building, unique selling propositions, ROI, R&D, and various other terms and acronyms. They may disagree on certain issues along the way, but at least everyone feels like they're speaking the same language. These meetings are usually quite lively. Everyone participates. At some point, though, there's one department in the agency that takes hold of the process and then translates all those "conversations" into the advertising itself. That department is the Creative Department. Ooooh. The CREATIVE Department. Just the sound of it is off-putting. Or highfalutin. A department for creativity. Everyone else sort of backs off from the process at this point in order to give these "creative" people a chance to be "creative." For the Art Director and Copywriter, the conversation continues, more lively than ever. They're mulling over the strategy, examining the facts, and creating the work in a sort of "incubation bubble." As suddenly isolating as this is, it's actually advantageous for everyone. Copywriters and Art Directors can get cranky if there's always someone looking over their shoulders. Clients, who can be intimidated by the "creative mystique," are often happy to yield control at this point in the process and wait for what comes out on the other side.

Business professionals aren't exactly sure what goes on in the Creative Department of an advertising agency. And that's understandable. There actually *are* things that happen in there that don't really happen anywhere else. For one, creative professionals have the uncanny ability to turn a strategic objective into a selling idea or creative concept. As it turns out, developing a creative concept is a very difficult thing to do, and the Art Directors and Copywriters who do it are both naturally gifted and trained in the discipline. It actually *is* a bit of magic when a narrowly defined business objective is transformed into a compelling message capable of changing the way the masses think. Indeed, this is why clients seek out agencies in the first place. So there really is validity to the "creative mystique."

There are two major pitfalls, however, to this period of isolation. First, it creates an "us" versus "them" mentality. In the extreme, this can result in a hostile work environment that's counterproductive. In moderation, however, this dynamic has a perfectly acceptable function. Creative people are often fueled by competition and a healthy disrespect for authority. They need to feel a good sense of "otherness" in order to justify their creative being. Therefore, the mentality itself is not a pitfall as much as how that dynamic is managed (which we'll discuss in the second half of the book).

The second major pitfall of putting the creative process into a bit of a bubble is that the work emerging from it seems a bit foreign to those not directly involved in its creation. Only a few short weeks ago, everyone seemed like they were on the same page. Now a few select people are off on their own working so uniquely, it's as though they're on another planet. How else could all that research, scientific data, and marketing analysis be turned into a colorful concept able to fit into the confines of a single page or a 30-second television commercial? Well, that's creativity in action. And to those unfamiliar with it, it can seem surprisingly alien. Of course, everyone is hoping that the big creative presentation will have an element of surprise; otherwise, the Creatives haven't done their job. But the trade-off to having this wonderful "voila" moment is that it's often followed by an awkward silence with clients sheepishly saying, "Can we get back to you on this?" It would be terrific if that simply meant the work was so good that words can't adequately capture the client's happiness. But that's usually not the case. Creative work just happens to be hard to interpret, difficult to judge, and tough to talk about.

Let's be clear: The "voila!" moment is good. And if it's followed by "eureka!" you've hit the jackpot. What's tragic, though, is that this powerful and desirable outcome often makes the process come to a screeching halt. If the business-minded people in the room don't know what to say during the creative presentation, a great opportunity for collaboration has been squandered. The moment for the business-minded people to reenter the process has been lost.

Here's the remedy. Everyone must be fluent in AdSpeak. What exactly *is* AdSpeak? It's a more comprehensive understanding of how those basic marketing terms are translated into the creative product. AdSpeak doesn't create new terminology. Indeed, it's a fairly small lexicon that's so basic and familiar, many terms are recognizable to the marketing-savvy consumer. When you first see them, you'll immediately recognize them from Advertising 101. But only knowing the textbook definitions is an illusion of knowledge. Without greater dimension, these words aren't enough to sustain anyone during a critique. So AdSpeak goes beyond definitions to reveal the deeper meaning and fuller expression of each term in action, that is, when embodied in the work itself. Creativity brings these words to life. By exploring this lively transformation, the terms take on greater meaning. Understanding that meaning allows every participant in the process to better evaluate the work. They not only have a more exact language at their disposal, but that language is now tied to something visual and concrete. This is what makes critique possible.

THE BASIC TERMS OF ADSPEAK: *They'll Change the Way You Judge Advertising . . . and Talk About It*

Even though Art Directors and Copywriters are the ones giving these words meaning, much of what they do is intuitive. Therefore, the link between language and outcomes is not easily articulated. Business-minded professionals use these terms with such fluency throughout the process that they don't fully appreciate how nonfunctional they are when evaluating the creative product. Hence, all parties know the vocabulary on some level—but not on the *same* level. Imagine the frustration of having the same vocabulary but not truly speaking the same language. Therefore, the objective here is to do a holistic exploration of these key terms—define them more deeply and then see them expressed in actual work—so that everyone involved is on the same page and can share the nuances of the language that will facilitate a more meaningful critique.

The Creative Strategy

AKA "The WHAT"

You know how people always tell you to "think outside the box"? Well, I hate that expression. I get the broader meaning of the phrase: to look for unexpected solutions that defy convention. Nothing wrong with that. But to me, advertising is all about thinking INSIDE the box. And advertising is full of boxes—or limitations, frameworks, and concrete realities. The budget is a box. The dimensions of the page are a box. The ingredients in the product are a box. The most important box of all is the strategy. If you can come up with a great creative idea that fits within the confines of the strategy, then you're a genius. Come up with a great idea that's wildly off the mark and NOT strategic, then you're an artist, not an advertiser—go mount an exhibit at the Met. This is not to say that you can't wail against the box. Or try to change the dimensions of the box. But at its very essence, advertising can only truly be advertising when it is a clear outgrowth of the box. The cleverest among us realize that the greatest fun of advertising is seeing how far we can go with an idea, an execution, a new media placement and *still be in the box*.

That's why we start our AdSpeak vocabulary list with that most important box of all: the strategy. This is probably the most basic term in the business. There are entire textbooks devoted to strategic development. And rightly so. It's critically important. So what is it? Simply stated, the advertising or creative strategy (sometimes called the creative brief) is a document, developed in partnership with the advertising agency and its client, that outlines *the objective* of the advertising *prior to its creation*. The strategy is initiated in response to this most fundamental marketing question: WHY? As in, why are we advertising? Once a key challenge and/or opportunity are identified, the strategy helps to *position the product* in the minds of consumers. It often does this by identifying the uniqueness or advantage of this product as compared to similar products that already exist in the marketplace.

The Four Basic Functions of an Advertising Strategy

1. To aid in the *coordination* of a more comprehensive marketing effort

This function is important to note because it reminds the ad agency that their client is working on marketing plans above and beyond the advertising. Ad folk sometimes think that they're at the center of a marketing effort. And even if that's true in some cases, the advertising does not happen in a bubble. Plus, in a 360-degree world, it's more important than ever for everyone to be aware of the whole marketing effort in order to be synergistic with it.

2. To get all levels of management in *agreement*

It would be wrong to say that strategies are static documents since there's always room for refinement. However, it shouldn't be a moving target while the creative team is generating the work. Why waste considerable effort and energy exploring ideas that will never be viable? So make sure that ALL levels of management have signed off on the strategy before creative development begins. This not only establishes a mutual starting point but forces people who aren't part of the day-to-day operations to get involved and become aware of the magnitude of any project. Sometimes a project doesn't seem "real" until a formal, important-looking document is generated. The strategy serves as that formal document. You'd be surprised how often the mere distribution of a formal strategy statement makes the project come to a screeching halt because someone who was supposedly "on board" actually reads the words on the page and realizes that this wasn't at all what he had in mind. Heads roll. Mayhem ensues. But it's better to crystallize issues at the strategic stage than to throw out some terrific campaigns that are already beautifully mounted but now horribly irrelevant. One final caveat: The word *agreement* can be subjective; most people are REactive rather than PROactive when judging creative work so be prepared for the strategic direction to be reconsidered AFTER the work is presented. Then you have to go through a whole new round of "agreements." But whether it's the first round or the twentieth, never, ever, EVER work on creative development until everyone signs off on the strategy.

3. To give *direction* to creative development

When people are asked what a strategy is for, this is usually the first thing that comes to mind. And with good reason. Copywriters and Art Directors need clear direction in order for their work to be strategic. Most people think that creative people hate strategies because they stifle their creativity. But here's the unexpected kicker: Good Creatives LOVE a good strategy. Why? Because the more smartly articulated the challenge, the more smartly articulated the solution.

It's just like when you ask a kid, "How was school today?" The question is so generic and broad that the most likely answer will always be "good." And unless you were being rhetorical, you haven't really learned anything about that kid's day. But if you ask, "Which question on the science test gave you the most difficulty?" or "Who did you sit with at lunch today?" then you're bound to spark a really fruitful conversation filled with detail and insight. Strategies are like that, too. When they're generic and broad ("to communicate that our peanut butter tastes better"), the work will also be generic and broad . . . and uninteresting.

4.   To aid in the *assessment* of outcomes

Interestingly, this is the function that most first-year students give little thought to. They're usually too fixated on the third function as though the strategy is merely a road map; once you've reached the destination, you can put it back into the glove compartment. Not true. It is this fourth function—which puts the strategy to use after the creative work has been developed—that is the absolute backbone of critique. Bringing the strategy into the creative presentation (mentally if not necessarily physically) and seeing how the work measures up to its objectives is one of the key responsibilities of agency account managers. Once you get into the "zone of creativity," it's the strategy that helps anchor the critique back to the land of the quantifiable and serves as the more objective filter for judgment. I often hear that "creativity is subjective," meaning that the only criterion for judging an ad's effectiveness is one's personal opinion. This couldn't be further from the truth. Assessing an ad through a strategic framework is a crucial element to determining whether an ad will work or not. For example, an ad campaign that you personally love may not be remotely effective if it is not strategic. And vice versa. The reality is that an ad is a complex mix of science and art, objectivity and gut reaction. So being articulate and specific about how the advertising works against strategy is what makes critique substantive and persuasive.

In the first three functions outlined above, the strategy exists as a discrete document, neatly formatted, typed, and easy to read. But in the fourth function, once the advertising's been created, the strategy has been transformed and is now embedded in the advertising. It's no longer a static text document; it's now actively doing its job in a way that the consumer can relate to. Creativity has made this transformation possible. Creativity has also made the strategy in this consumer-friendly form more elusive to the people who created it. This is where critique comes in to help everyone better assess whether the advertising is delivering on strategy. Here's how we start. Like many of the terms in AdSpeak, it's important to not only understand each term as thoroughly as possible but also distill them down to their truest essence so you can make clearer connections to the work. This helps us isolate the elements in an ad for easier analysis.

At its most basic, the strategy is the WHAT . . . as in: WHAT is the single most important thing that the ad wants the consumer to remember about the thing that is being advertised? As we've already discussed, a lot of research and thinking go into a strategy. A lot of elements make up a strategy. There are a lot of ways to format, phrase, and configure a strategy. But when you're staring at an ad trying to figure out if it's strategic, the most productive thing that you can consider is how well it answers this single question: WHAT is being communicated about the product? If your answer matches your communication objective to your satisfaction, you're in business.

Distilling the strategy down to "The What" also allows us to assess the effectiveness of the strategy as well as the ad. If, for example, we find that the ad is all over the place yet still strategic, we may begin to realize that the strategy is what's truly flawed. Advertising works best when it's razor sharp and focused. Knowing the essential meaning of our terms ensures that our critique tools are as sharp as the actual advertising itself.

The Strategy in Action: A Facilitated Critique—Altoids

Let's give the strategy for Altoids Mints a chance to speak to us through its campaign. Spend some time really scrutinizing the ad below and then ask, WHAT does this ad want us to know about the product? There is no body copy to tell us. No headline. The visual

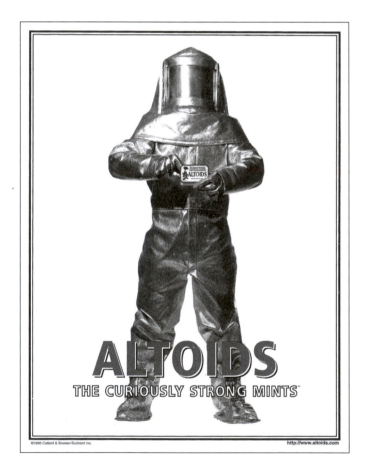

is striking, but straightforward—no real narrative or demonstration in the classic sense. Here's what we're seeing: a retro photo of a person in some sort of protective suit. But protective of what? Something dangerous? Toxic? We're not sure, but it must be pretty potent. And it's probably whatever he's holding in his hand: a tin of Altoid Mints. Once

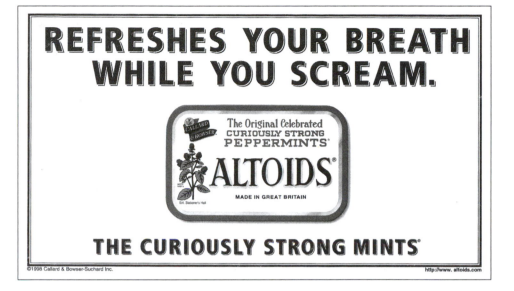

we read the tagline, "the curiously strong mints," we've taken in all the critical information that we need. And it all adds up to this "WHAT": Altoids are very, very strong. Is that this campaign's strategy? Yes, it is. Other brands may be trying to communicate how long their mints last (Breathsavers), how easy it is to get a quick hit of freshness (Tic Tacs), or how they make your breath more kissable (Certs). Altoids is strategically staking out the positioning that its mints are powerfully strong. The tagline tells you this, the packaging tells you that (it's made of tin, for goodness sake!), and so does its advertising. The same can be said about the two other ads featured here from this campaign. And despite the fact that the first one simply features the product and the second ad is for a line extension, "The What" is the same and clearly communicated in both.

No matter how you interpret these ads, one thing is clear: Altoids is one potent mint. In advertising, we'd call this campaign a great success. These Altoids ads are effective because they clearly know WHAT they're supposed to be communicating: potency. This message of strength is not just communicated in the collection of data points mentioned earlier. Potency is also communicated in the crisp visuals that have a strong personality. Potency is communicated in the fresh and dominant color of the background that will pop out of whatever media environment it's in. Potency is in the bold use of typography, the phrasing, the word choice. Nothing flowery here. Everything is right in your face. Therefore, creativity has taken this single strategic message and embedded it in nearly every aspect of the page. So when critiquing whether the ad delivers on strategy, we need to examine all aspects of the page, not just its major elements to see if they answer "The What" to our satisfaction.

The Strategy in Action: A Facilitated Critique—Bacardi

There are a lot of ways for an ad to go wrong. But its odds for success are increased by starting out with a smart, focused strategy. With such focus, the ad is able to deliver its singular message on the many levels in which advertising communicates. It bores down to make its point rather than making a big mess of itself. The chance for the reader to "get it" increases tremendously. The flipside is an unfocused strategy leads to ads that must deliver many different points all at the same time. This is not effective. Here's an analogy: Try throwing a dozen balls at someone all at once. It's impossible to catch a single one. In fact, the impulse is to give up, shield your face, and try not to get hurt. Absolute chaos. But throw a single ball directly at the target and chances are, he or she will make the catch. That's the difference between an ineffective ad with a fuzzy strategy and an effective ad with a focused strategy.

Here's a case to demonstrate this point. Let's look at two ads from the same advertisers but from different campaigns. Both are for Bacardi Rum but were produced a decade apart using different strategies. The first campaign, "Just add Bacardi," was introduced in 1992 and capitalized on Bacardi's Puerto Rican heritage. We get some of that from the headline in the blue sidebar on the left side of the page. But that's really just an isolated element added on to the main ad. Instead, consider the main strategic message contained on the right side of the page. By looking at this ad, WHAT do you suppose Bacardi want us to know about its rum?

Visually, there's a lot going on here. However, as part of a long-running campaign, most readers would have been quite familiar with the format: a main photographic scene of a serious situation that turns into something more tropical and fun in the spot where the Bacardi has been splashed. The image and headline/tagline, "Just add Bacardi," combine to communicate that Bacardi is responsible for this transformation. The strategic message, therefore, is that drinking Bacardi is like being on a tropical vacation. That's "The What" of this campaign. This is what Bacardi wants consumers to know about its rum.

The problem with this particular ad, however, is that the page is simply filled with too much information. First of all, the main campaign, visualized on the right, has "jumped the shark." In other words, it's trying too hard to communicate a simple message. The extremes are TOO extreme here. The man on the moon is so far from the ordinary that the consumer no longer connects to the message. But beyond this, the sidebar on the left adds information that competes with the main image. There are now two headlines on the page that use two different typefaces. One is bold and straightforward; the other looks like something from a science poster. Which should the reader look at first: "Bacardi. The world's great rum. Made in Puerto Rico" on the left or "Just add Bacardi" on the right? And isn't it confusing to be looking at a visual of a man on the moon while reading a headline that refers to the earth? Clearly, the advertiser figured that the sidebar on the left would just "borrow" a bit of real estate form the main campaign; who'd notice that the two messages don't quite work together? Well, the readers. They expect an ad to work as a cohesive whole. When it doesn't, the brain gives up and disengages. Why bother being confused when you can just look away? So rather than enhancing the ad, this extra bit of information turns the entire page into a communication mess.

After producing many ads in the "Just add Bacardi" campaign, Bacardi decided to move in a new strategic direction. Of course, this meant that they needed an all new campaign. Perhaps they saw the vacation mind-set as too restrictive. After all, not everyone wants to feel like they're on vacation at the end of a hard day. They just want to relax. So Bacardi came up with a new strategy and created the "Bacardi by Night" campaign. Here's one from that series of ads:

So where's "The What" here? We need to take in the main elements of the ad in order to figure that out. Let's start with the obvious: the belly button shot. It's not all that provocative to see body piercings these days. But the copy "Banker by Day" tells us that only hours earlier, this woman was dressed up in a corporate suit. Taken together, we're curious to know what's responsible for that transformation. The answer comes from the other half of the headline, "Bacardi by Night." Taken together, the campaign's strategic message is pretty clear: Bacardi is what you order after a hard day at the office and want to be your true, more relaxed self. That's "The What" that we want readers to take away from this ad.

Note that the tropical vacation strategy is no longer in evidence in this ad. The message is no longer about where the rum is from. It's has nothing to do with the fact that it's made from sugar cane and mixes well with other sweet things such as cola, pineapple juice, or coconut milk. There's no beach. Or splash of rum. The idea of transformation, however, is still a part of the strategy. But this time it's a bit broader than in the "Just add Bacardi" campaign. It's more open to interpretation. That's one reason why the photo is cropped so tightly: The close up of the belly button doesn't overdefine the target. That could be YOUR belly button that Bacardi helps to expose. It's provocative and intimate, yet still vague. The woman in the picture remains a mystery and open to interpretation. This is by strategic design. What does relaxation mean? That's up to you. It no longer means being on vacation. It no longer transports you to the Caribbean. After years of positioning Bacardi as a tropical alcohol, the tropics are gone. Bacardi's now got a seat at the bar, saddling up with vodka and scotch. Yet nowhere does this ad explicitly spell out that strategy. And yet the ad itself is very strategic. It resonates with consumers because it delivers the message through creativity.

The Target Audience

AKA "The WHO"

The target audience (or target market) is defined as the group of people who you think will be most receptive to your advertising message. This is not to be confused with the *consumer,* a term we throw around pretty loosely. The target is based on the marketing challenge or opportunity and refined in the advertising strategy based on what you want the ad campaign to accomplish. That means that the target audience of today's campaign may not be the target of tomorrow's—even if the product user remains constant throughout. For example, are your efforts trying to attract new consumers? Galvanize brand loyalists? Entice existing customers to use the product more frequently? Advance information about a product promotion or attribute? Enhancing or repositioning an existing brand image? Introduce a product extension . . . to new customers? Brand loyalists? And so on.

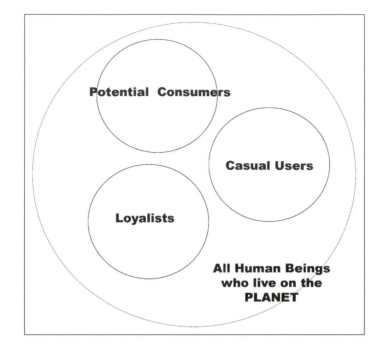

Since so many people use the terms *target* and *consumer* interchangeably, here's a chart to clear up the distinctions. The size of the outer circle is based on sheer population data and includes every member of the human race. Even when the marketing goal is to increase sales, we need to be realistic and acknowledge that not every product is right for everyone on the planet. Therefore, not everyone on the planet can be defined as "consumers." We need to be a bit more discerning. So let's look at the inner circles. The size of the two inner circles, "existing loyalists" and "casual users," is determined by sales figures. These circles are filled with our actual consumers. The size of the third inner circle, "potential consumers," is based on research that's determined who you think might have the greatest potential to buy your product but who currently isn't. So when you think of your product's consumers, you can narrow in on these three circles. However, these people are not necessarily our target. The target is up to you, the marketing expert. Depending on your marketing challenge, you can find your target in ANY of these four circles—although it's probably not cost-effective to simply aim your message randomly at the entire population of the planet.

The characteristics of your target audience are based on a demographic, psychographic, and geographic analysis. Distilled to its very essence, the target is "The WHO," as in WHO are we speaking to in this ad? WHO is on the other side of the ad? WHO needs to be motivated by and engaged in this advertising effort?

The target audience is one of the main elements of the strategy statement. But we isolate it here because a full understanding of "The Who" and how it is manifested in an ad is critical to critique. Knowing who you're talking to will undoubtedly affect the way that your strategic message is delivered. It will be embedded in both the substance and the style of the campaign. If an ad doesn't both capture and communicate with "The Who," there's no guarantee that the reader will want to pay any attention to "The What."

To fully appreciate this, I often tell students to imagine being at a lively, overcrowded cocktail party. You don't HAVE to talk to anybody you don't want to. It's all about who captures your fancy. Now say you've just bought a Harley Davidson and you're looking to strike up a conversation with people of similar interests. There's a good chance that you'll find yourself more attracted to the folks wearing leather than the ones wearing tweed. The operative word here is *attracted* because the cocktail party is a metaphor for how we engage in advertising. And ads are all about attraction—especially in a crowded environment where many things vie for the attention of a fickle and distracted consumer. So back to the cocktail party: In a sea of strangers, you're likely make a snap judgment. You might be wrong—the guy in the tweed might be the one with all the expertise on motorcycles. But that's okay since it's a cocktail party, and being wrong is of little consequence. People feel that way about ads, too. They're not hugely important to their lives. So it's that immediate connection that must attract. And it's the same sort of chemistry that you'd find at a cocktail party.

The Target Audience in Action: A Facilitated Critique—Dewar's

Speaking of cocktail parties, let's talk about scotch. In the late 1990s, Dewar's Scotch found itself in the middle of a magical marketplace moment. Times were flush. One of the economic engines of the era came from the rise of the Internet. The "dot.com" bubble was partly driven by a surprising segment of the population: young computer geeks in their twenties and thirties who had never before had their talents so richly or quickly rewarded. Being young and entrepreneurial, they preferred to go to work in blue jeans or pajama bottoms. Their work spaces often looked like romper rooms. Many were making so much money that they dropped out of Harvard or Wharton before they had their degrees in hand. It was great to be loaded and young! The only problem was that sometimes—not all the time, just sometimes—they wanted the world to take them a little more seriously. They displayed few of the visual cues that usually telegraphed success—no gray hair, corporate suits, or advanced degrees hanging on their wall. How could they stay true to youth and still let the rest of the world know that they had arrived?

Enter Dewar's Scotch. Up to this point, scotch had been traditionally associated with rich older men in oak-paneled studies who sipped it in front of a roaring fireplace. Or with high-level business executives who needed a strong belt after a bad business meeting. It's a fairly expensive hard liquor with a distinctive, acquired taste. Indeed, this explains the "old, wealthy guy" aura; it takes a long time to be able to both afford a bottle and acquire a taste for what's inside. So what would make Dewar's suddenly go after guys in their mid to late twenties? Because going to a bar and ordering a "Dewar's and soda" would be an easy way for dot.com entrepreneurs to telegraph their wealth and substance to the rest of the world. (This also accounts, incidentally, for the sudden surge in the popularity of cigars and fedoras.) So who exactly is "The Who" for this campaign? Fairly affluent men, 25 to 45, who are younger than traditional scotch drinkers but older than beer-chugging frat guys. Why bother ignoring your steadfast customers in this effort? Because Dewar's had faith in their loyal base and were thinking of the future. They could shift their focus for a short time period, seize a magical marketplace moment, and plant the seeds of loyalty. Rarely can a scotch aim so young without missing the mark.

So why not lower the target further and capture an even larger audience? After all, the drinking age starts at 21. The reason is clear: If the advertising were aimed too young, it would need to be louder, more boorish, and sillier. Think of the way that Budweiser speaks to college kids. Dewar's couldn't do this without diminishing the product's cache, which demands a sophisticated palate. So the target here is a delicate balance. This campaign may not have been aimed at their regular customers, but Dewar's had no intention of alienating them, either. That's why the target is so clearly and narrowly defined. See what I mean about a "magical marketplace moment"?

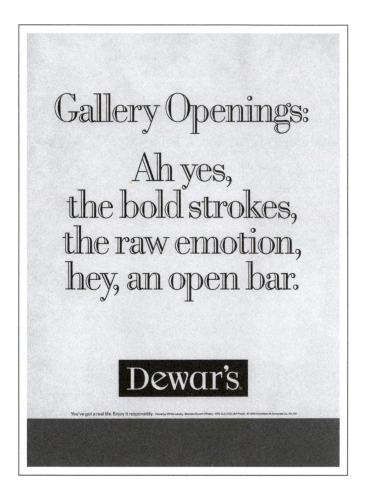

Now you know the background and have some sense of how the target audience is defined in the strategic document. But where is the target in the ad above? To the untrained eye, it may be difficult to assess because there's no photo of the target in the ad. Yet "The Who" is manifested in all sorts of ways. One way is through the tonality of the headline. Indeed, it is the voice of the target himself (remember, we're talking to men here). It's one side of a dialogue without the quotation marks. It has a certain wise guy quality to it without being juvenile. The person behind the quote is an emerging sophisticate, maybe even a poser who doesn't particularly care if he's exposed. After all, this target was born cynical; sudden affluence doesn't change that. In fact, it kinda reinforces it. Note the language choice; it is colloquial, yet not too slangy. It walks a fine line. Adding "dude" after the "hey," for example, would be going too far. Note also that in just a few words, we're IN situation. Even though there are no visuals, we see it all in our minds: a small gallery, a large crowd, a bar in the corner. It is a situation that is ripe for visualization, but the statement itself is so evocative, no visuals are necessary. It's an aspirational setting where culture abounds. Yet our target guy is more genuinely interested in the opportunity for a free drink. Again, this captures the exact moment in this target's life when he wants to exhibit the "trappings" of the moneyed class but can't yet emotionally measure up. And he knows it—hence the wink in the headline. Let's chart it out it:

"Gallery Openings: Ah, yes, the bold strokes, the raw emotion, hey, an open bar."

It starts with an establishing phrase, references that with an obvious cliché (i.e., those things you're supposed to say), and then exhibits a clear case of ADD as it's interrupted by a sincere observation and opportunity to escape (i.e., a drink). The fact that this drink is Dewar's scotch brings together the best of both worlds: desired sophistication and escape to "dudeness."

As added proof that creativity has transformed the term *target audience* and manifested it in an ad, let's remove the creativity and consider what the headline would sound like if it were a more literal expression of the strategy: "Hey, successful young professionals! Want everyone to think that your sophistication level is as high as your salary?" This embeds the target audience in the headline, too, but much more directly. It would be impossible to miss who the ad is trying to reach—which might make some clients very happy. But it also wouldn't be a particularly engaging headline. It is strategically clear but uninteresting. In addition, this sort of strategically obvious headline makes readers feel like marketing pawns being overtly targeted. They'd rather feel like they're part of a conversation about something that they're interested in. So the ad needs to attract their interest first and foremost. In this ad, the first step to that attraction is its conversational feeling. The ad is no longer just a piece of paper but the target come to life—sharing a moment with you, a likeminded pal. Imagine: no visuals of the target, no sound, yet it speaks to us with great animation. There's no doubt that the target is embedded in this ad. And there's no doubt who that target is. So being literal is not better. And it's no more true to the strategy than when creativity works its transformative powers.

Other elements of this ad are also creative translations of the term *target audience*. The typeface, for example, accomplishes many of the same things that the headline achieves. Remember how narrow our target is. So everything here must walk a fine line between not being stodgy but not too immature, either. The open-faced Caslon font is elegant yet has a modern feeling to it. The font says "grown up." The bold placement on the page says "risky." The colors help here, too. They relate to the Dewar's label, which is smart. But the way that they're used on the page also speaks to the target. The strong red and creamy yellow are boldly graphic as noticeable elements and not just as decoration. This pops, for sure, but also tells our target that this product is like them—straightforward, confident, strongly restrained, yet still colorful. Ultimately, "The Who" has a presence all over this ad. It not only speaks to the target but also is the manifestation of the target. Considering that this ad is also all about Dewar's Scotch, that's a pretty mean feat. But this is what's possible through creativity.

The Concept

AKA "The HOW"

This is one of the hardest terms to define yet the key to whether your advertising will be great or just wallpaper. A concept is a creative idea born of the strategy. It's also often called "The Big Idea" or simply "The Idea." As you can imagine, these words get thrown around a lot without full comprehension of their meaning. One reason is because the words *idea* and *concept* are part of our common language and in use everyday. But in the world of advertising, they have very specific meaning. Ad concepts are elusive; since they're abstract, they're easier to understand once they've been executed and are more concrete. Executions can be described, but ideas can only be articulated. Putting an ad concept into words is one of the great challenges for everyone, from Account Managers to Creatives. But defining and identifying a concept is probably one of the most valuable critique skills you can master.

George Lois, one of the first "idea men" in advertising, recently wrote a wonderful book called *The Big Idea* in which he defined a concept as "the shock of a thunderbolt that seemingly comes out of the blue (always a combination of thinking *and* intuition), the mythical and artful blending of context, image, words, and art can lead to magic, a juxtaposition of opposites that are dramatically connected visually. Concepts spring forth from the earth, and if they are big enough, are earth shattering. Great graphic communication depends on understanding and adapting to the culture, anticipating the culture, criticizing the culture, criticizing changes in the culture, and sometimes helping to change the culture." As one of the iconoclastic Art Directors of the Creative Revolution back in the sixties, you'd expect George Lois to be an eloquent champion of The Big Idea. But the invention of The Big Idea was not about showing off one's creative prowess; it was an act of survival. In the sixties, as advertising expenditures passed the $2 billion mark, Bill Bernbach (remember? He is a god to me) of Doyle Dane Bernbach determined that in order to cut through the clutter of competitive voices, a commercial needed to be distinctive. In order to be distinct, an advertiser needed to not just consider the content of the message but also the way in which it's delivered: through unique "concepts." Today, in the age of 360-degree advertising, The Big Idea is more important than ever. More clutter. More media options. More emphasis on brand building. The strategy, of course, is always critically important. But as Bill Bernbach would tell you, it's not just what you say in advertising; it's how you say it.

This brings us to that succinct definition of the term *concept* that will aid us in our critiques. The concept is "The HOW" as in: HOW is this ad delivering the strategic message? A single concept is the sustainable idea or overriding theme behind a campaign. It's what allows the particulars of each ad to change but for the campaign to remain the same. A concept is dynamic in that it forces the brain to do a bit of work in order to create meaning. An idea is often created through this equation: art + copy = meaning. It's YOUR job to add it up. Or figure it out. Unlike the strategy, which should lay out all its insights clearly and unambiguously, the concept is a bit mysterious. If it did all the work for you, you wouldn't engage in the ad. In this way, the concept is abstract; it doesn't exactly live in the ad. It lives in your brain. (FYI: The concept can be more elastic when leaving the print realm, but we'll discuss that later.)

The Concept in Action: A Facilitated Critique: American Floral Marketing Council

Once articulated, a concept can sound pretty simple—even if it's a stroke of genius. But it's not as easy to put into words as you might think. Even the person who spends sleepless nights giving birth to the concept will have trouble stating it plainly. The most important thing is to distinguish it from "The What." This is especially critical during a critique because unless you can't first identify the strategy, you can't measure the effectiveness of the concept you're evaluating. In the above ad, the *strategy* is to communicate that flowers are emotionally meaningful. HOW is this message delivered in the ad? The *concept* is to use the size of the arrangement to visualize how deeply you feel. Notice that this isn't a description of the ad, but the idea behind it. Also note that even though the ad itself is funny, the concept doesn't sound very funny. It sounds a bit dry and clinical. That's okay. It's the way that it's executed that makes it funny—and describable. So how does this concept come to life executionally? By asking a simple question in the headline ("How mad is she?") and showing three flower arrangement options. The reader doesn't need anymore information to get the joke: Sorry comes in three sizes. This ad is wonderfully strategic, conceptual, and executed simply, yet with universal humor. In other words, a great success. But before we go any further with more examples of advertising concepts, we need to more clearly understand how it differs from the execution. So let's move on to a definition of the execution, the next key term in AdSpeak.

Execution

It's often hard to distinguish between the concept and the execution. One reason is because many ads—even effective ones—are executionally driven. Since not all ads have strong concepts (and some have none at all), it's easy to get confused if you're looking for one. We're conditioned to believe that there's an idea behind every ad. That's why students will often squint at an ad for hours trying to figure out "the idea" rather than acknowledge that it simply doesn't have one. But whether an ad is conceptually driven or not, it always has an execution. Because an execution is what you're looking at. It's what ends up on the page. The execution is the way in which the concept is visually and verbally expressed. Executional elements of a print ad include the copy (headline/body copy/tagline) and the art (design/type treatment/visual components). A single concept can be executed many, many ways. That's because a concept is BIG and broad. An execution is more specific, yet must remain stylistically consistent within the context of a campaign. If the concept is the advertising's substance, then the execution is its style.

Every executional element on the page should play well with each other. The execution also needs to work really, really hard in many ways: to pay off the concept (if there is one); to deliver the strategic message; to connect with the target; to convey the brand personality; to make an impact all its own. That's a lot of work.

The more AdSpeak we learn, the more we appreciate how much an ad communicates on many levels, both discreetly and in relation to each other. When making a presentation on a piece of advertising, it's important to lay out those levels of communication in a fairly systematic way that mimics the process: You start with the strategy (including the target audience), move on to an articulation of the concept, and then describe the execution that works off of that concept. From there, the presentation can be more circular, doubling back over how one aspect relates to, supports, reinforces, or works off of another. A good critique works this way, too. First, there's the discussion of the linear progression from strategy to concept to execution. But then the critique doubles back and around, pulling elements apart and seeing how they relate to the whole.

While the execution is the most immediately visible thing about an ad, it's one of the last aspects that should be discussed during a presentation or critique. To the consumer, it's the only thing about an ad that matters. To the professionals, the execution is the outgrowth of a long process; you must have a sense of context in order to judge its merits.

The Execution in Action: A Facilitated Critique—Godiva

In order to critique the execution of the Godiva ad below, let's establish this ad's strategic framework and determine its concept. The strategy here is to inform upscale consumers that Godiva is an exclusive chocolate. At its most basic, this is WHAT this ad is supposed to communicate. HOW is it doing this? While this is not a heavily conceptual ad, a concept statement might be: "The idea behind this ad is to treat the product like it's a precious treasure." So let's move on to the execution. As with most things that are positioned as high-end, everything on the page must work very hard to deliver the strategic message. This ad is executed as a still life in which the products are photographed like jewels on the page. The headline, "Say it like you mean it," reinforces the importance of chocolate.

So what is it about the execution that tells us that Godiva is an exclusive chocolate? First, the product itself is displayed as a still life: Only a few are perfectly placed on the page, and they are beautifully photographed with delicate shadows. The background is a rich, textured gold with layers of overlapping type that read out a message so artfully, it's as much a part of the design as a text element. The headline, "Say it like you mean it," has a bit of wit to it, but it's not slapstick funny. The font is quite elegant. There's not much body copy; instead, the lusciousness of the product does most of the talking.

To illustrate just how hard the execution works to deliver the strategy, compare the execution of the Godiva ad to that of this ad from a long-running campaign that Ogilvy & Mather created for Reese's Peanut Butter Cups. Let's forget about the concept for a moment and stick strictly with the execution. Here's a description: The product is prominently featured on the page, but rather than looking like a still life or being in situation, the candy appears almost as a graphic element and in various stages of being eaten. The headline is handwritten and in quotes: "I eat them in phases." The quote is attributed to "Richard Chandler, Astronomer." The ad wraps up with a tagline, "There's no wrong way to eat a Reese's."

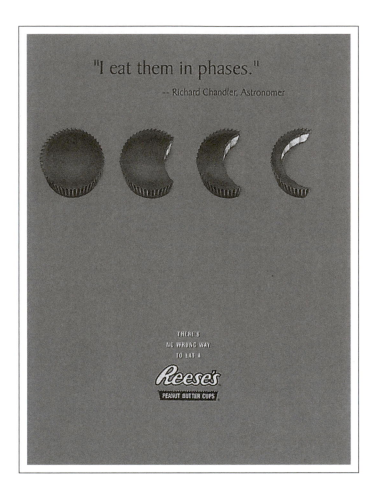

Without considering anything else about this ad besides the execution, name five things that communicate that Reese's Peanut Butter Cups are less exclusive than Godiva Chocolate:

1.

2.

3.

4.

5.

Here are some things that you may have included: The ad has no real dimension or texture; it looks flat—purposely so to mimic the colors of the Reese's packaging. The background color looks like something out of a crayon box; it's childish, not elegant. The candy on the page has already been eaten . . . not at all precious like Godiva. In fact, it looks like someone's been playing with his or her food. That's not something that would happen to an upscale chocolate. The headline is handwritten; this is very personable but not elegant. The tagline seems very inclusive: "There's no wrong way to eat a Reese's." On the other hand, the Godiva ad almost makes me afraid to pick up the product . . . am I worthy? The Reese's ad uses a more relaxed humor. It's clever but not witty.

If we went by the executions alone, ask yourself this: Which product would you give to your hostess as a housewarming gift and expect to be invited back? A box of Godiva? Or a Reese's Peanut Butter Cup? Clearly, the execution goes a long way to communicating a lot about an ad's product.

Despite the distinctions between the terms *concept* and *execution,* it's easy to get confused. So let's review.

Concept	Execution
Abstract—easier to articulate than to describe	Concrete—a manifestation that's "describable"
Broad—not tied to specifics	Specific—particular and changeable from ad to ad
Substantial—deep in meaning and sustainable	Stylish—the outward expression of the message

Executional Study: Reese's Peanut Butter Cups

Still unclear? Remember that a concept is big and can be executed many different ways. So to prove it, let's do a hypothetical exercise of the Reese's Peanut Butter Cup campaign. If the creative team had decided to go a different executional route, what might this campaign have looked like? Let's play around and take a look. Of course, we need to begin by identifying the existing strategy. Here's WHAT the message is: to convince adults that eating a Reese's Peanut Butter Cup is a uniquely fun eating experience. The WHO is folks with quirky tastes. So HOW are we going get this message to our audience? Basically, the concept is to show how people's personalities are expressed through the way that they eat the candy.

Keeping the concept the same, here are three different executional approaches. See which one you think best expresses the concept. The first ad is from the campaign that was actually produced and ran in national magazines.

Executional Approach Number 1

This execution expresses the personality of the eater by visualizing the candy after he's put his own personal stamp on it. As described earlier, the product is prominently featured on the page, but rather than looking like a still life or being in situation, the candy appears almost as a graphic element and in various stages of being eaten. The handwritten headline, "I eat them in phases." is attributed to "Richard Chandler, Astronomer." The ad wraps up with a tagline, "There's no wrong way to eat a Reese's."

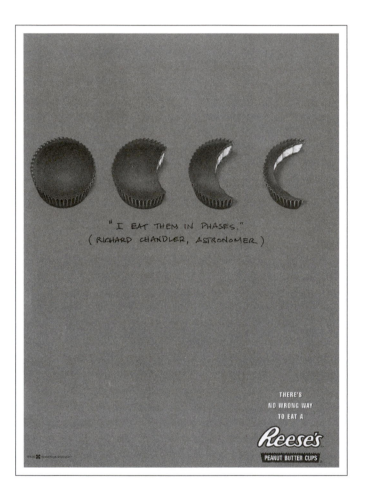

Executional Approach Number 2

In this execution, famous people are featured as they proclaim their personalized approach to eating this candy—an approach that is linked to their interesting professions or offbeat ideas. Here, the famous person is Galileo with his portrait centered on the page.

The product is eaten into a moon crescent which hovers above his head. The headline, "I eat 'em as I see 'em," is in quotes to indicate that this is Galileo's own explanation for why he chooses Reese's. The tagline is the same.

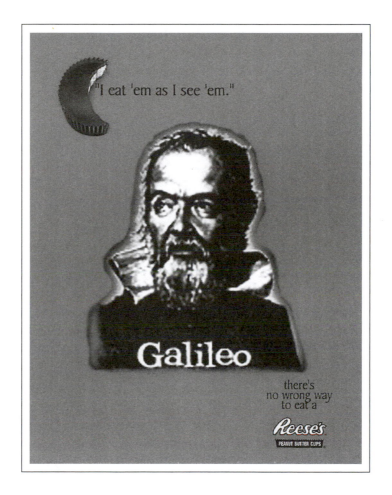

Executional Approach Number 3

In the third executional approach, the concept is expressed by showing the inspiration behind the featured individual's personalized approach to eating the candy. In this ad, the individual is once again Richard Chandler, a "noncelebrity" astronomer. He's not visualized in the ad, but the headline lets us know that he's the source of the pictured astrological chart that replaces the moon phases with the product in various stages of consumption. The headline, "Astronomer Richard Chandler's Approach (in phases)," is treated more as the caption of the chart than as a more prominent headline. The tagline is the same.

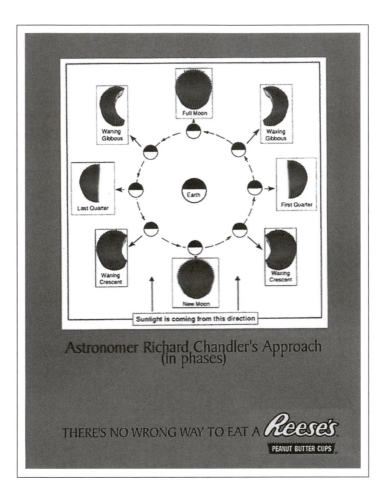

All three ads look different—too different to be considered all part of the same campaign. Yet they communicate the same strategic message. And they play off of the same concept. Of course, the agency only created the first execution and then followed that with a series of new ads that worked off the same concept and stayed within this executional style. By the way, are clients ever privy to such an executional exploration? Not really. By the time that the client sees a campaign proposal, its execution has already been hammered out. In fact, most creative teams don't even explore their own concepts in this way; they often come up with the concept and execution as a single bolt of inspiration. This hypothetical exercise is just to reinforce the meaning of these two important AdSpeak terms.

The Layout

The definition of the layout is pretty straightforward but can sometimes overlap with what we think of as the execution. While the execution refers to the style and content of an ad, the layout is how the elements of the execution go together on the page. Just as the finer aspects of the text are the domain of the Copywriter, the layout is truly the Art Director's territory. A well-designed layout is the final tipping point of communication. Every other part of the ad may be perfect, but with a misplaced headline or poorly chosen font, clarity may falter to the point of failure.

It's easiest to understand what a layout is by seeing a bunch of different ones for the same ad. Let's play with that Reese's ad once again. . . .

Here's the original ad. Layout elements include the placement of the headline, the product, the logo, and tagline, as well as the color and the typeface choice.

The alternate layout switches the order of the headline and product; there's a chocolate-colored band that breaks up the solid background. The candy loses a bit of its prominence here. Since the visual needs to do the heavy-lifting in terms of communicating the concept, this is a weaker page design.

The layout in the ad above features the product in a prominent way, but rather than a horizontal placement, the candy is "eaten" on a downhill diagonal. This has a certain drama to it—although some might argue that it's a less pure depiction of the passage of time than the straight horizontal placement. The real problem here is the headline's type-face. It's in a straightforward serif font that would seem to go with the casual nature of the candy. And it's easier to read. But it's also a bit boring. It's not as quirky as the handwritten headline in the actual ad. And since there is no person visualized in this ad, the headline has to work extra hard to communicate the person behind the candy. The fact that Richard Chandler is identified as an astronomer is critical. But so is the handwritten message; it's more personable. Just as this man makes a mark on the candy, his handwritten message leaves his mark on the page. Since the strategy demands that we communicate quirky tastes, the handwriting in the actual ad is clearly a better way to go.

> ## A Brief Message From Your Sponsor
>
> The strategic message. The concept. The execution. The layout. At this point, we've parsed the elements of a print ad—ad nausea. So what's the value of seeing these distinctions? Because during the critique, you really need to know specifically what it is that you're evaluating. And if you can't deconstruct all the layers of meaning, you're apt to respond too generally. This is fine if you're a consumer; he or she is allowed to love or hate something whole cloth. But if you're too vague during a critique, the process stops. Bad work has no chance of becoming better. The same goes for good work. (Question: Why *not* stop at "I love it"? Answer: because knowing *why* will help lead to loveable advertising on the next project.) Now that you've learned that the concept isn't the same thing as an execution or the layout, your comments can be more specifically actionable. You can distinguish between loving a concept and hating an execution. Now you're less likely to allow a beautiful execution to seduce you away from appreciating how ineffective the strategy is. This is the real beauty of understanding AdSpeak: You can pull an ad apart and figure out which parts of an ad are effective and which aren't—rather than throwing out an entire campaign because you can't quite figure out what's wrong—or right.

Campaign

Tomato ketchup in a bottle. None'll come and then a lot'll.

—Ogden Nash

A campaign is a series of ads or commercials that is driven by a single concept. Each ad in a campaign should have its own impact while remaining true to the basic, overall concept. Mounting a successful campaign is advertising nirvana. A campaign is a way for consumers to immerse themselves in your message. With a single engaging concept and consistent executional approach, a campaign allows you to experience the same strategic message in different ways and in difference venues. It's redundant without being repetitive; familiar and fresh at the same time. A campaign can span a period of time. The longer a campaign lasts, the more interactive it becomes. Once a concept's premise has been established, each ad has a built-in awareness that makes us immediately connect to it—whether we like it or not. Our minds begin to make relative judgments: Is this a better execution than before? Is it funnier? Our minds begin to look for subtle differences: What's new? What's added? Subtracted? An orphan ad doesn't invite these kinds of questions. In a campaign, each ad not only communicates on its own but has a cumulative effectiveness that results from the campaign's focused and increasingly familiar thinking. Campaigns build a relationship with the reader. The first ad that you see may make no sense. Perhaps the second or even third ad in the campaign doesn't click for you. But by the fourth, you not only understand the ad but also come to like the campaign (we often confuse familiarity with appeal). By the fifth ad, you get real excited and start to look forward to the sixth . . . when will another one come out? Sometimes clients don't have the patience to stick with a campaign. But it's like the ketchup bottle. If you believe that the first few hits determine the outcome and don't wait for the big payout, you'll end up with a dry burger.

The Campaign in Action: A Facilitated Critique—California Milk Processor Board

In a way, a campaign not only works off a single concept but proves that you've got one. The dramatic simplicity of the original "got milk?" ads launched in 1994 by Goodby, Silverstein & Partners for the California Milk Processor Board helped establish this as one of the most recognizable campaigns in advertising history. This campaign is also a great teaching vehicle for clarifying the differences between a concept and an execution as well as defining what a campaign is.

We can really appreciate the strategic message of the "got milk?" campaign for two reasons. First, because so much has been written about it. Second, because the message is so clear in the advertising itself. Distilled down to its essence, the WHAT of this campaign is: Milk is uniquely satisfying; indeed, when it's paired with certain foods, nothing else will do. Focusing on milk's supporting role is not only a better way to get consumers to appreciate the value of milk but also a good way to ensure that you won't run out . . . or you'll be sorry. What makes this a particularly powerful strategy is that Goodby, Silverstein & Partners figured out a way to give milk a sense of urgency—no easy feat given that milk is a pretty low-interest product.

But HOW can the ads themselves get consumers to appreciate this supporting role? Through an absence of milk. And HOW do we communicate milk's absence? By *only* featuring foods that are usually paired with milk; this way, we'll crave what's missing. To instill an even greater sense of urgency, each food item has a single bite taken out of it— as though the consumer couldn't resist sinking his teeth into that cupcake or that cookie. Only when we see the words "got milk?" artfully placed near that tasty bite do we fully realize that milk isn't part of the deal. Suddenly, we've never wanted a glass of milk so much in our lives. We appreciate just how uniquely satisfying it can be. The concept doesn't just get us to understand the strategic message; it makes us experience it. All without ever seeing a visual of milk. Amazing, eh? A milk campaign that doesn't show milk. Yet clearly communicates "Don't run out . . . or else."

The print ads in this campaign are simply executed in a way that really brings the concept to life. Each ad focuses on a single food item, such as a cookie or a peanut butter and jelly sandwich, that would be unthinkable to eat without a tall glass of milk. The foods are graphically photographed against an all-white background in an appetizing close-up that fills the page so that the consumer is focused only on the food; indeed, it seems as though it's right under his nose. The tagline, "got milk?" is always as close to the bite as possible.

Seeing the series of "got milk?" ads on pages 41–42 not only helps define what a campaign is but also brings to life these three other AdSpeak terms: the strategic message, the concept, and the executional approach. It's impossible to miss the cumulative power of a campaign here. You wish there were more ads. And you can't help wondering, what's next? Each of these ads has its own strength in delivering the message. But the repetition of the idea with different particulars makes the message particularly compelling and believable. The ads are fresh the first time you see them yet also familiar. You're already bonded to the concept before the next ad comes out.

The Campaign in Action: A Facilitated Critique—Absolut

A conversation about campaigns wouldn't be complete without discussing the campaign that introduced Absolut Vodka to America. Cited by *Advertising Age* as one of the 10 "Best

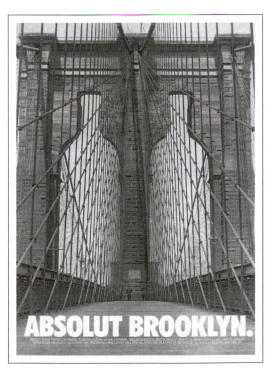

Campaigns of the 20th Century," it ran for over 25 years. Each ad was like a small puzzle, challenging—and certainly engaging—the reader to make sense of the art and copy elements in order to determine the ad's full meaning. Yet they always added up to the same thing: perfection as defined by Absolut. Some were wildly successful. Others faltered. But that's one of the beauties of a strong campaign; weak ads can be forgiven as long as you deliver enough of the good stuff. For decades, people not only loved these ads but also collected them. They even looked forward to the next one (imagine . . . actively seeking out an ad!). What other advertising could inspire a coffee table book with a collection of nearly 500 ads from the same campaign?

When this product was introduced to America in the 1979, the marketing goal was to introduce a Swedish brand of Vodka in a way that distinguished it from the dominant vodka brands from Russia. The key was to not just make the distinctive shape of the bottle instantly recognizable but to communicate that WHAT was inside the bottle was perfectly pure. So the conceptual HOW of this campaign plays with the bottle in such a way that, when coupled with two words, "Absolut BLANK," the ads create a definition of some form of perfection. There is no better demonstration of how "art + copy = meaning" than the Absolut vodka campaign.

In each execution, the bottle (or its shape) is photographed as the hero of the page. It is manipulated or contextualized in some way. The headline (which also doubles as a modular tagline) always sits boldly and graphically underneath the image so that the art and copy read together. Hundreds of ads later, this campaign adheres to the same strategic message, stays true to the same concept, and only rarely deviates from its basic executional approach.

As with most established campaigns, the more ingrained it becomes in the consumer mind-set, the more elastic the execution can be. One pitfall to that, of course, is if the audience really loves you, some of the loyal purists can get peeved—not a bad problem to have!

The Campaign in Action: A Facilitated Critique—Bombay Sapphire Gin

To really nail home the definition of a campaign, here's one more that'll help make it crystal clear. This one's for Bombay Sapphire Gin. The strategic message is pretty straightforward: to convince drinkers that Bombay Sapphire Gin is uniquely exceptional. Unfortunately, this message is not particularly unique or exceptional. But fortunately, it was brought to life by an effective concept: Bombay commissioned renowned artists, craftsmen, and sculptors to create one-of-a-kind martini glasses. Why? Because the gin is so uniquely exceptional, no ordinary glass will do. Each ad is executed like a still life: The lighting is dramatic. The colors are softly subdued. The bottle of Bombay Sapphire Gin acts as a backdrop for the true work of art–a specially designed glass filled with a perfectly poured martini. Together, these ads don't just make up a good campaign, they make the strategy look good.

Campaigns are a great way to reinforce the same strategic message over a period of time, especially if you have a sustainable concept that consumers will continue to find interesting ad after ad. That's the case with the Bombay Sapphire campaign. The first two ads shown here were produced when the campaign first ran in 1992. In the second set of ads on the next page, Bombay manages to freshen up the campaign with a more stylized execution that is still faithful to both the concept and the strategy.

Tagline

A tagline or slogan is an enduring catchphrase that positions the product or the company. Famous examples include "Just do it" for Nike, "Be all that you can be" for the Army, and "A diamond is forever" for DeBeers. Sometimes it acts as the pedestal that the company sits upon or as the distillation of the product's unique selling point or as the summation of the advertising concept that drives the campaign. It can sometimes stand alone. Sometimes it makes no sense unless an entire ad comes before it. About a decade ago, Volkswagen introduced its tagline by setting it up with a "pre-tagline": "On the road of life, there are passengers and drivers. Drivers wanted." Once the campaign was established, they dropped the setup and just went with "Drivers wanted." A campaign is bonded by a single tagline. However, sometimes a tagline is so well known, it will outlive the campaign that spawned it. Sometimes, it ends up where it's least expected. Here's an example of that.

"Got Milk?" Versus "Where's Your Mustache?"

In the mid-1990s, two separate campaigns for milk were launched. One was first seen regionally on behalf of the California Milk Processor Board and carried the tagline "got milk?" As critiqued earlier, this campaign is the epitome of success: conceptually flawless, pitch perfect, and commercially effective. Every element of this campaign works extremely hard. And nothing works harder than the tagline. "Got milk?" is the succinct summation of the campaign's message and captures it with a sense of urgency. One quick question. Two short

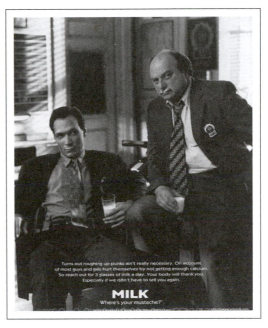

words. The hope, the desperate hope, that the answer is, yes! Yes, I do have milk! If the campaign did not end with "got milk?" we'd be left feeling incomplete, waiting for the other shoe to drop. We might even miss the point entirely. Need proof? Take your thumb and cover up the tagline. Does the ad make sense any more? No, it does not. In fact, this tagline delivers so much information that it practically has the status of a headline AND a tagline. Combined. Today, this line is extremely well known and lives independent of the campaign while still carrying the message of the campaign concept. It's probably among the most well-known taglines in advertising history. But it needed the campaign to give it meaning.

The other milk campaign was created by Bozell Worldwide for the National Fluid Milk Processor Promotion Board. The very first ad in this long-running campaign featured a portrait of supermodel Naomi Campbell shot by famed photographer Annie Leibovitz. It looked like a typical fashion shot except for the fact that Naomi sported a mustache of milk above her upper lip. This was followed by thousands of other ads featuring celebrities of the hour wearing a milk mustache. The campaign was immediately well received by consumers and remains popular today. The strategy is pretty broad: Milk is for everybody. The concept is pretty straightforward: By leaving telltale traces of milk on celebrities, the campaign proves how far-reaching milk consumption is. Unlike the "got milk" campaign, there's no need for a tagline to complete the communication. The milk moustache tells the whole story. So it ends up with a less important role. In fact, since its inception, this campaign has had three different taglines. The first was "Milk. What a surprise!" The second, "Where's your moustache?" lasted a bit longer. It was a solid tagline that reinforced the action on the page." As a question, it invites readers in. It's short and to the point. But it doesn't resonate like "got milk?" because it's not integral to the campaign's communication. "Where's your moustache?" is an interesting afterthought. "Got milk?" seizes upon that moment of desperation that the campaign creates.

While the moustache campaign has many fans, it was not the marketing success of the "got milk?" campaign. However, it's still going strong, featuring recent celebrities such as Taylor Swift and Beyoncé. So in an effort to achieve some of the effectiveness of "got milk?" this campaign did an amazing thing: It dropped its second tagline and adopted a third. You guessed it. The tagline is now "got milk?"

This unusual turn of events creates an interesting case study for us. It begs the question, are taglines truly interchangeable? Is "got milk?" so powerful that is works just as well in the National Fluid Milk Processor Promotion Board's campaign? Does it make it better? We know that it's become part of the cultural lexicon and is instantly recognizable, even unattached to an ad. So has it helped the effectiveness of the moustache campaign? Yes and no. It still does a lot of heavy lifting, but in a different way. In the original campaign, it helped complete the message and add meaning to the visual. Here, the campaign message doesn't really rely on the tagline for meaning; however, it does take advantage of the line's independent power, which, in turn, transmits some of the insight, urgency, and fun of the California Milk Processor Board's campaign into the milk mustache campaign.

"Just Do It" Versus "Planet Reebok"

Perhaps one of the most powerful taglines of the past few decades is "Just do it" for Nike. Created by Weiden + Kennedy in 1988, the line is so beloved that it's become part of the vernacular. In fact, when they tried to kill "Just do it" a few years ago, public outcry resurrected it. It's been around for so long and so poorly mimicked that we've begun to take its value for granted. We've also begun to read into this line a lot more than these three words intended. But there's no doubt that it encapsulates a brand personality that's allowed Nike to become one of the world's largest resources for athletic shoes and apparel.

Just what's so great about it? "Just do it" is a command. The "just" signals that we're closer than we think to getting off our butts. That's tough love. It pushes us off the couch and into the gym. Or on the courts. Or the running trail. Or wherever. It's not dictating what it is that we should "do" as long as we become active. "It" let's us decide that for ourselves. At no point does the tagline demand that we buy a particular product. We don't feel like we're being sold to. Indeed, we're somehow grateful to Nike for this kick in the pants.

Structurally, the line is no nonsense, rhythmic, and direct. It moves forward, linearly like an athlete sprinting toward the finish line. No extra clauses or descriptors. It is goal oriented. Each word is short, sparse, a pop in our mouth. There's nothing flowery here, yet it has its own poetry; compact like haiku and full of interpretive meaning. It's a pithy punch—less talk, more action. It's broad, yet personally motivating; it feels like it's intended for me while not alienating anyone who's not me.

When Nike ran the first ad with "Just do it," Reebok was the market leader. But a few years later, Nike was breathing down its neck. Reebok responded by trying to capture the cool that Nike was not just instilling in its product but in its advertising. The "Planet Reebok" campaign, created by Chiat/Day, hit the airwaves in 1993. Asking consumers, "What is life like on Planet Reebok?" it featured extreme athletic activities and concluded by stating, "No excuses. No lawyers. No winners. No losers." It was punctuated by the tagline: "Planet Reebok." While this affected a certain attitude, the campaign didn't have Nike's authenticity and ultimately fell flat. "Planet Reebok" embodied the tone-deaf nature of the campaign. It was corporate-centric rather than consumer-centric. There was no athleticism to it. This was a place, not an action. It sounded passive and alienating. Who wants to live on Planet Reebok? In response to this, the tagline evolved into "This is my planet" in 1995 and was soon dropped entirely not long after.

Both these examples reveal the communication potential of the tagline. It can embody the message, be a conceptual element, or bond together the campaign. Or it can feel like a few obligatory, thrown together words at the bottom of the page. You choose.

THE MORE ADVANCED TERMS OF ADSPEAK: *Sharpen Your Tongue . . .*

Brand Identity and Equity

People relate to brands, not companies. But what exactly does that mean? If a company has clearly communicated who it is using consistent products, messages, tone, and imagery, it develops a brand identity. This is what captures the imagination of consumers, not the company's spreadsheet, its bricks and mortar, or research and development. Without a brand identity, the company doesn't exist in consumer consciousness. Clearly, then, it's important for a brand to create a brand identity and build awareness of it.

Brand equity works a lot like a savings account—or at least how your grandparents described how a saving account worked. With each consistent brand-building effort, brand identity gets solidified in a consumer's mind. It's built up bit by bit and over time; then one day, you realize you've got something substantial and sustainable on your hands. That's equity, and it can be found in many different elements of brand identity, such as an attribute, symbol, message, even a typeface that comes to represent and encapsulate that product/corporation in consumers' minds. It requires a lot of exposure, a certain length of time, and meaningful quality to build up brand equity. But when done well, it's an instant read for consumers with built-in meaning. That not only makes equity a powerful communicator, but representative of power itself. Having equity means you're established and important. Once in a while, you can flaunt it and, like that savings account, cash in on some of that equity. But you've also got to protect it by constantly contributing to the equity bank. That's because equity is hard to build up but easier than you think to bankrupt through lack of support or weak communication. Elements of brand identity that have a lot of equity include the swoosh for Nike, the lion for Dreyfus, Mountain Grown® coffee for Folgers, and the cowboy (and the color red) for Marlboro.

This series of ads exemplifies the power of brand identity and equity. Before revealing the brand, examine each ad and see if you know who the advertiser is.

Glamour

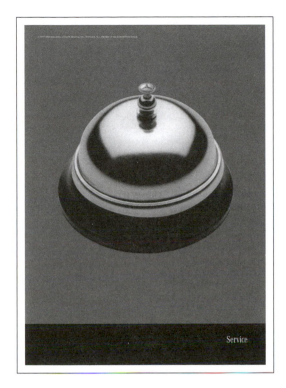

Okay, did you guess? About a third of the people who look at these ads know who the advertiser is. That's amazing since there's no product being visualized. No company name. And if you're in the third who guessed, you probably feel pretty smart for figuring it out. This means that a company has the ability to make you feel smart without overtly selling you anything. Doesn't that make you feel good about the company? And how were you able to identify the advertiser? Through your own observational skills and the power of equity. In a sort of "Where's Waldo" puzzle, the product is represented by its logo, which appears discreetly in each ad. If you missed it before, now go back and look again. See it? Look in the butterfly wing. Marilyn Monroe's beauty mark. The thingy that you push down on the service bell. See the tri-star logo? Now you've got it. So who's the advertiser? Mercedes Benz, right? If a significant portion of readers can figure out that these ads are about Mercedes Benz without seeing a car, then that tri-star logo, which is part of Mercedes Benz's equity, is pretty powerful. And that tells you something about the power of their brand. Of course, Mercedes can't keep running ads like this or else the logo will begin to lose its meaning. But once in a while, ads as oblique as this really do demonstrate the sheer power of the brand. Which in turn enhances the brand equity.

"Ownability"

Whether your advertising is conceptually or executionally driven, its success will depend on how "ownable" it is. In other words, are you the only company that can justify your positioning, look, and feel? Usually these qualities are rooted in the distinctiveness of the strategy, but "ownability" can also be found in the smallest details. During critique, a good question to ask is, Can we "own" this ad? That's one of the gold standards of effective advertising. If you don't have it, you become part of the wallpaper. Here's proof:

The next few ads appeared in the same newspaper section of *The New York Times* that ran one Sunday called "Education Life." The first three ads were for different

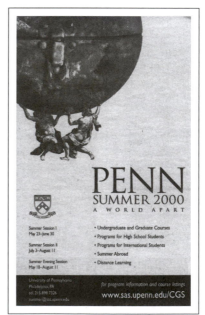

universities that all felt that they offered a world-class education. While this is most certainly true, the problem is that many universities can say exactly that. And all three did. In their ads. In the same publications. On the same day. As a result, it was hard to distinguish one ad from the next. Which meant that these three universities came across as virtually the same institution. But Columbia University isn't at all in character or content like St. John's University. And neither is the University of Pennsylvania. However, that would easily be the net takeaway for consumers who were reading the newspaper on this particular Sunday.

Now take a look at the fourth ad from Pratt University. This ad has something "ownable" to say. It featured a sculpture from George Segal, a renowned artist and Pratt graduate. The headline, "I Made It," references both the creation of his art and his professional success. The tagline, "Build it. Create it. Make it," speaks not just to the school's particular expertise but to its outcomes. Together, no other ad in that section on that particular Sunday could've looked anything like this ad. It was "ownable" only to Pratt. And that's the difference between standing out and looking like part of the wallpaper.

Brand Personality

Capturing a brand's personality in an ad is critical to any branding effort. That's because ads don't just deliver information about the brand, they represent the brands themselves. This means that our feelings about a brand often originate with or are reinforced by the way we relate to its advertising. Simply stated: Companies and products are physical entities; brands exist in the hearts and minds of consumer. And how does it exist in a consumer's heart and mind? One way is by actually experiencing the product or service. Another way is by authentically experiencing the product or service through the advertising—which means that an ad cannot just convey information about the brand, but must capture its personality as well.

The essence of a brand's personality can often be found in the company's vision (i.e., what singular value it's adding to the universe, society, our lives). For example, the Italian design company Alessi doesn't sell tea kettles; it adds poetry to your life. Starbucks isn't about gourmet coffee; it's about providing affordable luxury to everyday people. Kodak isn't a film company; it creates memories. Elements that reflect or symbolize the vision, such as logos, typefaces, and colors, make up a brand's identity. That identity is often expressed through a personality that is amplified by advertising in order to develop a relationship with the consumer. If a company doesn't have a vision, elements used to create an identity have no real meaning. This makes it difficult to create a brand—like a person with no personality. Of course, a company or product can still advertise. But the results are more short-term and concrete.

So how does the brand express its personality in an ad? A great example is Volkswagen, which has had a pretty consistent brand personality since it introduced the Beetle to America back in the sixties. Doyle Dane Bernbach did such a good job establishing a brand identity for this quirky-looking German vehicle during the postwar brand boom that it still prevails in the hearts and minds of American consumers. It has faltered over the years, but is regains its footing when it sticks to that core essence: fun functionality. Or maybe a bit more broadly: non-elitist engineering. This is clear with the famous "Think small" ad of 1964 as well as the relaunching of the Beetle more than 30 years later.

Let's take a look. See if you can recognize Volkswagen's brand essence in the "Think small" ad, created by Doyle Dane Bernbach in 1963.

Fast forward more than 30 years. By looking at the spread right below it (created by the Arnold Agency), what do you suppose Volkswagen's brand essence is? Same thing, right? Fun functionality and non-elitist engineering.

Despite many different models and advances in engineering technology, the brand essence hasn't changed. The cars are different. But the brand isn't. These two ads—more than 30 years apart—help tell this story. The particulars on the page differ, but the personality is pretty much the same. Which tells you something about how much of a brand's personality is delivered through advertising. Here in the United States, our initial perceptions of that weird little car were based on the advertising that introduced it to the masses. Before the average person saw the original Beetle on the street, he probably saw it in an ad. Or in a commercial. The advertising framed the reality so instead of seeing an object, the consumer reacted to a personality. The ads didn't just give voice to the personality; they helped shape it. So much so that 30 years later, both the new Beetle and the ads that "re-introduced" it feel like old friends.

As first established back in the sixties by DDB, the Volkswagen brand personality is communicated on both a conceptual and executional level. The idea here is to use the car as an ironic icon—it doesn't look like a conventional car, which gives it permission to function in ways that you wouldn't expect. Executionally, both of these ads isolate product. No winding Pacific coast roads. No beauties slung over the hood of the car. Just the car itself against a seamless background. The Beetle IS a weird-looking car in the context of the automobile market here in the United States. But by not hiding behind any props, the ads acknowledge this on your behalf. The car isn't just weird-looking but small—especially to

American eyes. The ads actually accentuate the smallness. This gives the car a measure of pride; it's not embarrassed by its smallness, so why should you be? Immediately, then, we start assigning personality traits to this object. It speaks to us from the page.

Now onto the text elements. When juxtaposed with the visual, the headlines ask you to realign your thinking. This gives you permission not only to acknowledge the car's quirkiness but to also consider how that quirkiness can work for you. The ads playfully deflate some of that hyperbole so often used to sell cars. This lets you relax. Yet the facts are quite serious about the engineering. This validates the seriousness of the purchase. The typeface is modern but not sexy. Again, a confident choice that almost mocks more conventional typography found in this category. When you consider the brand essence and then see these ads, they are one and the same. And that's a good thing.

Page Personality

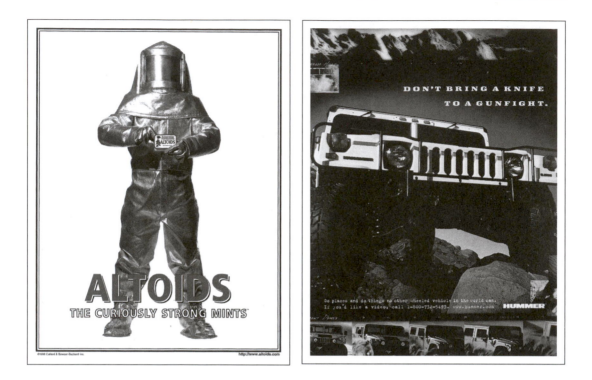

An ad can't just capture the personality of the brand; the page must have a personality of its own. Why? Because it must stand out among all those other forms of advertising that constantly bombard the consumer. The real trick is making these two personalities one and the same. When all of the elements of the execution work together to create an effective, emotionally powerful print ad, it seems to come alive with a personality of its own—a personality that should be consistent with, *as well as* help convey, the brand personality. This is truly the domain of a great Art Director. But as someone in the critique seat, you must also be able to recognize its importance when evaluating the work. The ad might deliver every single bit of communication demanded by the strategy, but if the page has no pizzazz, it will all be for naught. Here are a couple of examples where everything on the page comes together to deliver the strategic message and the brand, all at the same time.

Altoids is a great example of advertising that communicates its strategic message of strength in a brand-consistent, yet unexpected way. One of the less obvious elements that creates page personality is the powder blue background. A strange choice to telegraph strength. Yet it has meaning on many levels. For one thing, it makes the visual pop. And gives it a clinical harshness. In context, the color looks frosty rather than wimpy. The starkness makes it stand out—whether the ad is on a phone kiosk or in a magazine. If the Art Director had described this ad rather than showing it to you, you'd be skeptical that making pale blue a dominant element of the page would deliver on all of these things. But seeing is believing.

Another great example is the Hummer ad. The car nearly breaks off the page. But rather than use some gimmick to do that, it's just about the car itself, some bold photography, and good cropping. The page is powerful in the same way that the car is—a bit boxy and rugged. In this way, the brand personality is reinforced by the page personality. Supported by a strong headline in no-nonsense type, the ad has stopping power all its own.

Demo

AKA "The Proof"

This is a real basic term that's easy enough to understand but difficult to execute with real believability. We are sophisticated consumers skeptical about all forms of advertising. Yet despite the hokey quality of most demos, we're still fascinated by them. Why else would

we watch infomercials about really sharp knives until way past our bedtime? But do we truly believe them? Doing a side-by-side comparison while screaming into the camera doesn't work for many products. We are dubious, on one hand. On the other hand, we want the claims to be proven, verified, and authenticated. So how do we bridge this divide? We need to find ways to create convincing demos that balance cleverness with credibility.

The ad for Ivory Snow detergent is a terrific example of how a straightforward, side-by-side comparison can be engaging and convincing at the same time. The headline is clever and sets up what we're looking at. But it's mostly the contrasting sweaters that do all the talking. It's an attractive ad without looking fake. And somehow, the elegance adds to the believability.

The campaign concept of the above ad for Polaroid actually revolves around the notion of "proof" and brings to life one of the great axioms of advertising: "Don't say it, be it." In other words, advertising works best when it doesn't just deliver a message, but dramatizes the message. This is exactly what Goodby Silverstein did in its campaign for Polaroid. The ads don't include a demo; they ARE the demo. Here, Polaroid is positioned as a sort of "proof machine." And so the concept behind the campaign is to offer up the photos as the proof necessary to validate various situations. The situations are fun and engaging and embedded in real life. But the demos are on clear display nonetheless. In this way, the ads demonstrate the power of Polaroid by *being* demos. If that explanation sounds a bit confusing, the ads are not. They're clear, engaging, and convincing. We immediately appreciate the value of instant photography. That's why the invention of digital photography was such a hit. Unfortunately, it also made the Polaroid camera fairly obsolete a few years after this campaign was launched. Advertising can't save everything. . . .

The Terms: A Cheat Sheet

Brand Identity and Equity: How a brand is made evident and sustains value

Brand Personality: The characteristics of a brand brought to life—often through advertising

Campaign: A series of ads based on a single concept

Concept: The HOW as in "How is this ad delivering the message?"

Execution: The way in which the concept is manifested

Layout: The way in which the elements of an ad are designed on the page

Ownability: A positioning, identity, and style that make an ad unique

Page Personality: How an ad comes to life

Proof: Demos that are believable

Strategy: The WHAT as in "What does this ad want us to know?"

Tagline: A pithy phrase that captures the essence of the campaign

Target Audience: The WHO as in "Who is this ad talking to?"

 Visit the student study site at www.sagepub.com/tagstudy for additional online resources including web links, video clips, and recommended readings to learn more about advertising and the creative process.

Critique Exercises

1. Select five "good" ads and five "bad" ads (i.e., effective and ineffective) from magazines you might not usually read. Deconstruct in terms of each ad's WHAT, WHO, and HOW.

2. Go to http://www.textart.ru/database/slogan/list-advertising-slogans.html and select three taglines from the same product category. For each, identify the strategy and list five reasons why the tagline is effective. Consider the mechanics of the line as well as the message.

3. The MPA Kelly Awards were established in 1982 by the MPA (Association of Magazine Media) and are bestowed annually to agency creative teams and advertising clients whose magazine campaigns demonstrate both creative excellence and campaign results. Pick an award-winning campaign from the Kelly Gallery (http://www.magazine.org/advertising/kelly_awards/kelly_gallery/index.aspx) and list at least 10 ways in which the brand speaks through the ads.

4. Select favorite campaigns from the Kelly Gallery. Articulate the concept of each campaign and then describe the execution of the ads.

5. The Advertising Education Foundation (AEF) has a case study of Levi's integrated campaign that won an AME (Advertising and Marketing Effectiveness) Award in 2006. Go to www.aef.com/exhibits/awards/ame/landing to enter the exhibit. Review the Levi's campaign and read the case study. Pull apart the ways in which the campaign has "ownability," relies on Levi's brand identity and equity, and exhibits both brand and page personality.

6. Reexamine the concept behind the "How mad is she ad?" on page **29**. Keeping the same concept, execute this ad another way.

Suggested Viewing

If you ever want to see the exact moment in a creative presentation when a client doesn't know what to say, watch the first scene of the John Hughes's movie *Planes, Trains, and Automobiles* as the client (played by William Windam) silently debates the merits of a print presentation while the agency reps (played by Steve Martin and Lyman Ward) squirm in their seats realizing that with each second of silence, they're closer to missing their plane ride home to Chicago.

Suggested Reading

Twenty-Two Tips on Typography by Enric Jardi. You don't need to be a typographer or an Art Director to appreciate how every little detail in an ad is a communication opportunity.

CHAPTER 3

AdErrors

When Good Ads Go Bad

We're surrounded by horrible advertising. Every day. All the time. So why include more here? Because deconstructing ads to figure out why they've gone bad is one way of figuring out how to make ads good. As you'd expect, advertising can falter in many ways and at different points in the process. Sometimes it's the smallest detail. Sometimes it's a sweeping mistake. A single bad ad can contain many errors. But all it takes is a single error to undermine an ad's effectiveness.

Here are 13 classic AdErrors that block communication, diminish interaction, and essentially turn an expensive media buy into wallpaper. The problems are pretty common. But this will give you the language to critique work that you just knew in your gut was bad. Once you've got these 13 errors down, you can look at every stage of the process and determine what went wrong, how to fix it, and when to just toss the work in the trash.

AdError One: The Headline and the Visual Are Redundant or Disconnected

An effective headline does many things; reiterating, explaining, or describing the visual is not one of them. That's what we'd call "see-say." On the other hand, make sure that the headline doesn't ignore the visual, as though the two were totally separate entities. Magic happens in the interplay between headline and visual. No interplay, no magic. Be on the lookout during the concept stage, although it's most apparent in the executional stage.

Example: Cask & Cream

This ad is a great example of art and copy redundancy. The scenario depicts a couple of hounds delivering slippers and a newspaper to their master as he sits in a big, comfy leather

chair sipping a Cask & Cream on the rocks. It's the classic cliché of indulgent, decadent living. The visual couldn't be clearer; there's no room for misinterpretation. But rather than work off the obviousness of the visual, the headline simply repeats it: "Seem a bit indulgent?" The worst part is, the ad includes a subhead just in case we couldn't figure it out: "Now you're catching on" (nudge, nudge). It's a quintessential see-say followed by an insult!

Here's a simple rule: Don't do this. Instead, do this: If you don't feel that your visual is communicating what it needs to, then change the visual. The purpose of the headline is to work *with* the visual to create meaning. Don't make the mistake of using the headline to "fix" the communication. Don't treat the headline as just an afterthought. Once, my Art Director joked that my words were ruining his ad. It was a joke. We laughed. Then got back to the serious business of making art and copy synergistic.

AdError Two: Meaningless Gimmicks and Borrowed Interest

We all want people to stop and look at our advertising. But if that stopping power has no connection to the product that we're selling, then that power is fleeting, ultimately ineffective, and perhaps even a turnoff.

Borrowed interest means that an ad is using a compelling communication element or detail from somewhere other than your product or strategy. A meaningless gimmick means that the attention grabber doesn't have anything to do with the message. Bottom line: Work harder to figure out what's interesting about your product and make that the central communication. Usually a conceptual problem, but could happen in the execution or even the strategy.

Example: Oscar Mayer Bacon

Whoa. A bacon fence. This certainly does attract your attention. But to what end? Perhaps the headline holds the answer: "We go to great lengths to bring you America's best bacon." Hmmm. Oh, now I get it. The fence is long. So this represents "great lengths." Actually, no. I don't get it. Do I now know more about Oscar Mayer and its expertise as a result of this ad? Isn't that what the strategy wants me to know? If so, then this ad falls way short. It does get my attention. So kudos to the food stylist who put this together for the photo shoot. But an effective gimmick should not only grab your attention but also deliver on strategy. If it doesn't do both, the creative team has a lot of explaining to do.

How do ads like this happen? Usually because the creative team can't find anything interesting to say about the product. They fear that no one else will be interested, either. So they try to find something, *anything,* that will make the reader look at the ad, such as a bizarre gimmick, borrowed interest, or bacon fences.

Did You Hear the One About the Traveling Salesman and the Meaningless Gimmick?

A gimmick is defined as a "trick or device intended to attract attention, publicity, or business." While I don't defend using trickery in advertising, there's nothing wrong with trying to attract attention to your product or service. Indeed, that's our job. But advertising has to work harder than merely attracting attention. Here's an illustrative story about a traveling salesman. . . .

Years ago, long before television pitchmen and infomercials, many products were sold door-to-door by traveling salesmen. One product that lent itself to this form of selling was the vacuum cleaner. But as with any product sold door-to-door, the biggest hurdle was getting people to not slam the door in your face. One gimmick that vacuum cleaner salesmen used was to knock on the front door with a handful of dirt. As soon as the "lady of the house" opened the door, the traveling salesman would throw the handful of dirt onto the floor. Naturally, the housewife would be shocked. While a dozen thoughts may have raced through her head, the prevailing one would be: Clean this mess up! Of course, the salesman would have the perfect solution. He'd take out the vacuum cleaner that he was selling and suck up the dirt faster and more effectively than she could have ever imagined. She'd be impressed. Her anger would turn into curiosity, which might eventually turn into a sale. Amazing, huh? We can probably all agree, then, that this is an effective gimmick. It got the customer's attention and led to a purchase.

But not so fast. Let's say that this traveling salesman was not selling vacuum cleaners but toothbrushes. The gimmick of throwing a handful of dirt into the foyer would have still attracted the housewife's attention. Her initial response would have been the same: Clean this mess up! Unfortunately, all the salesman would have to offer was a toothbrush and the promise of cleaner, whiter teeth. She would've slammed the door in his face or sent her husband out to punch him in the nose. Or both.

Same gimmick. Two results. In the first case, the gimmick was closely tied to the product and the selling message. It worked. In the second, the gimmick certainly attracted attention, but it had no connection to the product and failed to hold the consumer's attention. Not only was the sales objective not achieved, but there's a good chance that no one in that household ever answered the door for a traveling salesman again. The lesson is clear: Gimmicks can be great, but if they're not meaningful, you'll not only fill the world with worthless gimmicks but end up eating dirt.

AdError Three: Using Spokespeople Who Are Irrelevant to the Product or the Message

Don't have an idea? Put a celebrity in your ad!.The irrelevant use of celebrity is a toxic combination of meaningless gimmickry and borrowed interest. Plus it's so overdone that the impact is often nil. Qualifies as an AdError when it masquerades as an idea . . . but it's really just an idea-less execution.

Example: Sub-Zero

Okay, I admit it. This is the ad that inspired my quest to identify the most common errors that sabotage advertising. When I came across it in a magazine, I practically fell off my chair. Aside from the nice portrait of Amelia Earhart, there is nothing good about this ad.

It's filled with so many errors that it's hard to isolate them. However, the most obvious is its misuse of celebrity. What does this fallen aviator have to do with an upscale refrigerator? Maybe my confusion can be explained away by the headline: "Because I want to." Hmmm. I had actually just purchased a Sub-Zero for my home, so this message was especially puzzling to me. The Sub-Zero is a very expensive, very impressive piece of machinery. It's so impressive that calling it a kitchen appliance would be an insult. Purchasing this piece of equipment for your home requires much more consideration than just because you want to. So the headline doesn't clarify anything. Totally baffled, I have now shown this to my students every semester and asked for their help: What do they think the connection is between Amelia Earhart and Sub-Zero? So far, we haven't come up with anything definitive. This ad is so befuddling that even the suggestions sound like questions: She was a renegade and so is Sub-Zero? She never returned from her last flight, but Sub-Zero is always there for you? If she were still alive today, a Sub-Zero would be her appliance of choice? Opening a Sub-Zero is like flying a doomed airplane? My favorite response is pretty far-fetched but just as plausible as anything else: She's dead and maybe this would be a great place to store her body? Send your suggestions to me. We'll crack this puzzle yet.

AdError Four: Lack of Focus

Variety may be the spice of life, but it's the death of an ad. The more information you cram into a single ad, the less ANY of it will be absorbed. For impact, you need power. For power, you need focus. Focus. Focus. Think narrow, not wide. Think pithy, not verbose. When's the last time you got talked into *feeling* something? This flaw can often be traced back to the strategy, but lack of focus can dull any stage of the process.

Example: Kitchen Basics

Hey! I've got a good idea! Let's run a bunch of messages of equal value up the flagpole and see if anyone salutes. Wrong. That's a bad idea. And the ad above is a really, really bad ad. Let's list all the discrete pieces of information that this ad wants us to know: "Rich & Dark,"

"Heart Healthy," "Like Homemade," "The key ingredient to many recipes, such as: Risotto, Chicken Sauté, Classic Pot Roast, Turkey Chili, and Carrot Soup." That's a lot of stuff. But if you read the body copy, there's even more: "Why settle?" "11 great tasting flavors," "New in 2009! Heart Healthy! The American Heart Association has certified three of their flavors"—hence the Heart Healthy logo on the carton, in case you didn't already know. There's so much info going on in this ad that it doesn't even speak in full sentences, just a lot of bullet points. Of course, the clients love its product. And well they should. It's great. In fact, this is the brand I use to make *my* risotto. However, the agency does not do it justice by simply using the page to park a litany of product attributes. Combine this with perhaps one of the blandest visuals of a product imaginable, and this ad is a waste of money. It's so out of focus that it's invisible.

AdError Five: The Page Is Overdeveloped and/ or Poorly Planned

Yes, the page is expensive. But it's like real estate—its value goes *down* when overdeveloped. An ad's competition is not just the clutter other ads but editorial content. What could possibly stand out more than restraint and simplicity? Also, have faith in the attraction of good design—an ad that's attractive *attracts*. And remember: White space *is* power. Blame this one on the layout, although the execution sometimes instigates it.

Example: Conair

Simply a mess. There's so much stuff crammed into this 8.5 × 11-inch ad that the eye doesn't know where to go. Even that coupon isn't enough to hold your attention. It's easier to just turn the page, which is what you're about to do right now. . . .

AdError Six: Sacrificing Clarity for Cleverness

Being clever is mandatory. But when it comes at the expense of clear communication, it's not good advertising. This can usually be straightened out in the execution unless an over-reaching concept is at fault.

Example: Birds Eye

This ad is working very hard to make a fairly mundane product interesting. The problem is that the visual is too clever for its own good. It gets in the way of clearly communicating what Chicken Viola! is: a frozen pasta and vegetable dinner that includes chicken. The headline acknowledges this by offering up a cutesy explanation for the inner tube and goggles: "Chicken Voila is making quite a splash." Eventually, you might get it. But none of it really makes sense. A chicken about to jump into a pool isn't an easy metaphor for a frozen meal that comes to life in a skillet. But you get the sense that everyone from the Creatives to the client thought that this image was so funny, it didn't really matter. It does. It does matter. Be clever—yes! But be clever *smartly*. It takes a bit more brain power, but that's what it takes to create effective advertising.

AdError Seven: Overacknowledging Your Competition

It's good to be competitive. But don't let the central idea of your advertising be *about* your competition. It gives them a free plug and defines you by what you *aren't* instead of what you *are*. And that's pretty lame. Competitive strategies that are taken too literally and expressed too blatantly will need to be fixed in either the concept or executional stage.

Example: Smirnoff

First, a history lesson on vodka. Virtually unknown in the West until a Russian refugee named Vladmir Smirnoff sold the formula back in the early 1900s, Smirnoff became the brand that defined the category here in the United States. Indeed, it's the brand that made vodka one of the most popular distilled spirits in the country. Even now, it is still the number one selling vodka. However, the greatest growth in the past decade has been the sales of super-premium brands, such as Absolut, Grey Goose, and Finlandia. Taking action, Smirnoff responded with the above campaign from its ad agency, Lowe Lintas, which ran in the late 1990s. The tagline "ALL VODKA. NO PRETENSE.," takes direct aim at the brands nipping at its heels. While not mentioning its competitors by name, headlines such as "This new vodka is filtered through sand imported from Scandinavian fjords. They say it's so pure it can almost pass for water," make it plenty obvious. But in the process of denigrating the "upstarts," Smirnoff takes the spotlight away from itself. Even worse, the brand looks defensive and even a bit scared; these ads tacitly signal that the competition is doing well enough to build an entire campaign around them. Not a good position for anyone to take, but an especially risky strategy for a leader.

AdError Eight: Letting Your Strategy Show

An ad can't be too persuasive if its audience is too aware of its methodology, research results, advertising objective, target audience, and so on. People need to connect to ads viscerally. That other stuff's about as persuasive as a saltine. Plus it can be pretty transparent (and then we're painfully aware that we're looking at advertising). This problem is usually seen in the executional stage . . . often because the advertising has bypassed the concept stage altogether.

Example: Myrtle Beach, South Carolina

This ad looks like someone just cut a few lines from the strategy statement and pasted them into a piece of paper along with a few stock photos. Even the most effective strategy shouldn't be confused with a good ad. While it may make sense to position Myrtle Beach as affordable (and what vacation shouldn't be "fun-filled"), to simply state it as plainly as that couldn't be any less engaging. True, the message is unambiguous. Unfortunately, it's also flatfooted.

AdError Nine: Being Edgy for Its Own Sake

When the effort shows, it's distracting at best and laughable at worst. "Hipness" is risky because it's inexplicable. One hundred percent authenticity, in both style and substance, is a must. You're either edgy or not. Trying doesn't count. This AdError can rear its ugly head in the executional, layout, and even production stages.

Example: Smith Micro

Wow! Look at that edgy typeface. See that cool dude with the totally awesome haircut and wild hand gestures. Read that headline: "You've got personality." Hey, they must be talking to you: a young, hip student—because who's got more personality than you do? Unless it's the totally cool dude in this ad! Wait a second . . . that's not how the target is going to respond to this ad. At best, they'll quickly turn the page. At worst, the ad will strike them as repulsive as a substitute teacher trying to be your best friend.

AdError Ten: Huh? Using Pretzel Logic, Being Too Subtle or Obtuse

No one should have to suspend reason or work too hard in order to comprehend an ad. And if you think that bad puns and cute copy can explain away tortured contrivances or elusive nuances, think again. Ads that are a stretch and strain are a big pain in the neck. Who needs it? An execution that tries to make sense of a complicated concept will often fall for this AdError.

Example: Ricoh

Seeing the master of surrealism being sucked down into a funnel is an interesting visual—surreal, even. But what does Salvador Dali have to do with copiers? Think about it. Do you really want your next copy to come out as absurdly distorted as one of his paintings? Okay, so maybe I'm interpreting the visual too literally. Maybe Salvador Dali is meant to personify the sort of renegade thinking that Ricoh would like its brand to represent. So let's read the body copy for some clues: "When others were creating copiers, we created the first digital copier that could copy and fax. And while others were creating copiers that could copy and fax, we created the first digital copier that could copy, fax and print." That's pretty cumbersome copy. Plus, it lays out a leadership argument in a very concrete and flatfooted way. Perhaps the visionary part comes later. Let's read on: "You might mistake one of our Aficio copiers for a Dali masterpiece, but that's just because we've always been a little ahead of our time." Hmm. Mistake a copier for a Dali masterpiece? Is that because it's all melt-y like the clocks in "The Persistence of Memory"?

Trying to figure out what Salvador Dali has to do with Ricoh copiers may be lots of fun for an AdError exercise, but no consumer wants to waste time doing it—especially if all that effort isn't rewarded with a reasonable answer.

Salvador Dali's masterpiece, *Persistence of Memory.*

AdError Eleven: Forgetting About the Product

Too often, advertisers get distracted by irrelevant information or sensationalism. So distracted, in fact, that they forget to communicate what's compelling about the product itself.

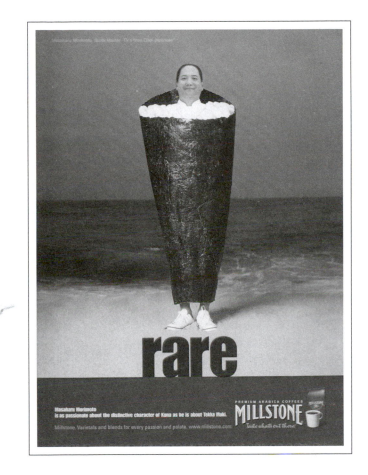

Example: Millstone Coffee

The biggest surprise here is *not* that Chef Morimoto is wrapped in a sushi roll but that this is an ad for coffee. Generally speaking, coffee is not paired with Japanese cuisine, especially tekka maki. So it's not just a strange spokesperson choice but a doubly odd visual. If the point here is to compare Morimoto's rare skills as a chef with the rare quality of Millstone Coffee, then why wrap him up like sushi—which is raw, not rare? It seems as though the creative team or the client got so excited about meeting their favorite Iron Chef that they forgot that the product they were advertising was a complete mismatch.

AdError Twelve: Being Boring or Too Obvious

Unless it's about a cure for insomniacs, an ad shouldn't put you to sleep . . . it should captivate the brain and galvanize you into action. In addition, effective advertising is interactive. It should do most of the work for the reader . . . but not all. If the brain doesn't engage, the reader feels cheated . . . and unmotivated. Every stage—from strategy to production—can fall victim to this AdError.

Examples: Northland Juice and Cetaphil

Here are two clear examples of this AdError. The ad on the left-hand page communicates that Northland juices are 100% with a headline that states that they're 100% juice against a backdrop of 100% real fruit and that's pretty . . . boring. And if you want to be really obvious about being a doctor-recommended product, then create the ad like the one below that features a doctor "speaking" directly to camera with a headline that begins, "I tell my patients. . . ." Zzzzzzz.

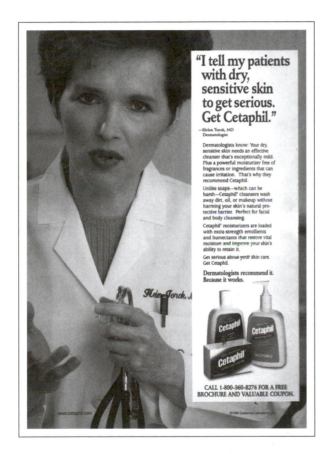

AdError Thirteen: The Tonality and/or Visual Style Is Inconsistent With the Product or Message

Even tried-and-true advertising devices will not be effective if they aren't compatible with your image, product, service, or benefit. Plenty of clients will come to briefings with examples of advertising that they like. "Can we do something like that?" they'll ask. Sometimes, a creative team will see a cool typeface, visual style, or tone in an award-winning ad and want to replicate it for their next project. But you can't pick a style first and then apply it to a campaign if it's not in sync with the message of brand personality. You can usually *see* this misstep, which means it lies in the executional, layout, or production stage. On the other hand, an ill-fitting strategy or concept could be the culprit right from the get-go.

Example: NicoDerm

Here's our final AdError in action. If your strategy has decided to focus on your product's calming method to break the cigarette habit, then *make* your ad calming. Don'T SHOUT YOUR MESSAGE IN ALL CAPS. As Marshal McLuhan said, "The medium is the message."

That means that the typeface should express the message as much as the words themselves. As anyone who text messages or e-mails (i.e., everyone) can tell you, all caps means shouting. Bold type means bold communication. And one more thing: Don't feature an action shot of the ex-smoker. If this product were truly effective at calming him down, then he shouldn't look like he's rushing to catch a train.

 Visit the student study site at www.sagepub.com/tagstudy for additional online resources including web links, video clips, and recommended readings to learn more about advertising and the creative process.

Critique Exercises

1. Go through magazines you otherwise wouldn't read and find an ad to illustrate each AdError. Bring to class, mount to wall, and have others match the ad to the AdError.

2. Find three examples of celebrity spokespersons who are strategically smart and three that are irrelevant and distracting.

3. Analyze the Sub-Zero ad and write a 200-word essay on your best guess of what the strategic message is. Vote on the class winner—it's anyone's guess.

CHAPTER 4

AdAnalogy

How Art and Copy Play Together

Robert Mankoff, the cartoon editor of *The New Yorker,* once said, "Everything I need to know about creativity I learned from cartoons." Cartoons have a lesson for us, too. Of course, nothing is less funny than explaining a joke. But this will be worth it. No other form of communication parallels the way a smart, single page print ad works quite like a single-panel cartoon. So analyzing how they work is a great way to fully appreciate the operational elements of a print ad. And that's a great way to increase your critique skills. So let the instruction begin—and feel free to chuckle along the way.

Why Are Single-Panel Cartoons Funny?

For starters, let's define what a single-panel cartoon is. Pick up any issue of *The New Yorker* magazine and you'll see single-panel cartoons sit alongside poetry, film reviews, and art openings. Or look at political cartoons featured in newspapers. Or buy a collection of cartoons from people like Gary Larson or Glen Baxter. Most single-panel cartoons comprise a simple line drawing coupled with a pithy caption. In the ad biz, we'd call this "art & copy." As in a good print ad, these cartoons often rely on the synergy of text and visual to create new meaning. Their humor also relies on the juxtaposition of familiarity and surprise. The joke must be understood quickly but not instantaneously; the reader must first take in all of a cartoon's elements—the visual, the caption, the overall style, the subtlety of gesture—as well as their interrelation with each other. This is a speedy process, but a process nonetheless. But then "wham!" The cumulative effect hits us over the head. It's an epiphany. It's *funny*. And despite all of that brain power, it feels like a gut reaction.

Consider your own thought process to the cartoon below by Peter Steiner and write down the order that you took in the top five pieces of information.

"Need anything from the bank?"

Write down what you looked at first:

1.

2.

3.

4.

5.

Usually, the first thing you look at is the visual, especially noting anything that's out of the ordinary. Of course, first you have to absorb what's ordinary before determining what stands out. In this case, you probably immediately registered this as a mundane domestic scene but then noticed the slightly unusual presence of a ski mask on one of the main characters. From the details, you get the sense that this is a married couple in their home. Maybe the husband's heading out for a winter jog? Yet you know it's a cartoon, so you figure that there must be something else going on. The picture is drawn in a childish manner but not really funny in its own right. So you figure the answer must be found in the text. By itself, the caption sounds pretty familiar: "Need anything at the bank?" You may have said something like this yourself—"Need anything at the store?" Or "Can I get you something while I'm out?" So it doesn't sound out of the ordinary. But then you put the text and the visual together and suddenly the whole scenario looks different. The ski mask no longer looks innocuous. It's now pivotal to the humor. Is this is a bank robber who's also a thoughtful husband? Or a thoughtful husband who probably shouldn't go anywhere near a bank? Either way, it's funny. The text and visual play together to create humor in a way that each element didn't have on its own. And you chuckle. And that makes the joke a success.

Of course, the process is a lot faster than the time it takes to read about the process. The brain is an amazing thing. Nonetheless, there was a fair amount of brain power expended. But this must be balanced by the fact that you shouldn't have to exert a whole lot of effort to understand the joke. Otherwise that all-important "wham!" is more like a "thud." The humor is diminished or lost altogether. On the other side of it, if the cartoon is too obvious, it's not funny at all. It's more like a statement of fact. Which means it's no longer a cartoon. Then the reader is left wondering what he or she is looking at.

Therefore, a cartoon must have a degree of complexity—a twist, a turn, a play on words—in order to be humorous. Alexander Pope once said that wit is "what is often thought, but ne'er so well said." A good cartoon is like that, too. Knowing its potential to entertain, we're seduced. It's tough to pass one by. We see it. We pause. We linger. We are willing to invest a little bit of ourselves . . . because we expect a relatively large payoff: a chuckle, maybe even a chortle. But despite the small investment, the stakes are high—no payoff and we feel ripped off. The moment of truth lives in the balance. With just the right degree of complexity, we feel entertained and, on some critical level, smart. Without enough complexity, the cartoon isn't funny and we're disappointed or even angry. With too much complexity, it's oblique and we feel stupid. All this just goes to show the extent of our emotional involvement with mere images and words on a page. A good cartoon, like a good ad, is a very powerful thing.

Funny? Unfunny? How Cartoons Work

All this explanation is great. But here's proof. What follows are two versions of the same cartoon created by Robert Mankoff that help to illustrate this lesson. The first one is manipulated in order to *not* be funny. That's right. It's NOT funny. The text has been changed from the original. It has been rewritten to support the visual in a descriptive, concrete, and expected way. In this version of the cartoon, the text serves the same function as a caption under a newspaper photo. It is redundant because it repeats what the visual is communicating. In the ad world, we'd call this a classic "see-say." In other words, you're seeing what the text is saying. Without a framework for analysis, there's nothing wrong with that. But if we were to measure this cartoon against a simple objective—to make people laugh—we'd have to agree that it's a real failure because *it's not funny.* The original version of this cartoon appears next. And it's funny. But don't look until you've fully appreciated how "unfunny" the first cartoon is.

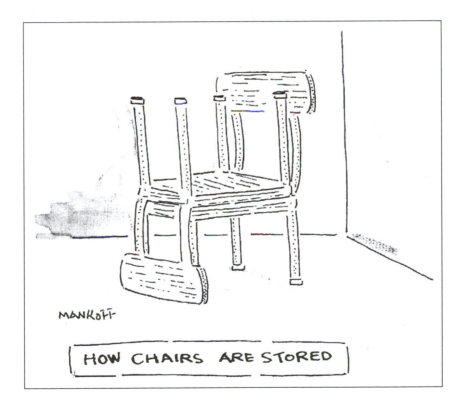

Not funny, right? Okay, now look at the original cartoon on the next page. You'll see. It's funny.

See? Now this is funny. And since we can assume that Mankoff's goal was to be funny, this cartoon can be considered a success. But how does it achieve its humor? It starts with the synergy of visual and text; they work together to create new meaning. Then there's the interesting juxtaposition of familiarity and surprise that catches us off balance. We've all seen chairs stacked up like this. It's an incredibly ordinary sight. But do chairs have sex?

It's probably never crossed your mind before. But if they DID have sex, this *might* be the way it looked. There's a logic at work, but not the outcome that we'd expect. And at its core, there's an insightful truth . . . didn't you always wonder why there were always more chairs in the classroom after a long weekend? The cartoonist, Robert Mankoff, suggests that this cartoon represents a parallel universe where "pieces of furniture strike pornographic poses." That's pretty funny in and of itself, but you don't need to analyze it to that degree in order to find this cartoon funny. It's much simpler than that. Yet complex at the same time. All in a single panel.

Here we go again, only this time let's play with the visual rather than the caption. The unfunny version of this cartoon by *New Yorker* cartoonist, Tom Cheney, is below. In it, we see a typical scene in which a waiter asks a customer how his food is. Nothing out of the ordinary about that. And nothing particularly funny about this version of the cartoon, either.

"How's everything?"

However, let's now look at the actual cartoon. The scenario is essentially the same: a man eating dinner as the waiter checks on him. The caption hasn't changed, either; it's the same in both versions. This time, though, it's the visual that's changed and is out of the ordinary. Instead of a regular-sized meal, the diner has a ridiculously high mountain of food on his table. In fact, the visual is now more literally in sync with the waiter's deadpan question, "How's everything?" because now the diner does indeed seem to have every possible food item in front him. What's funny about this is that a phrase we hear all the time is now being suddenly applied to the absurd—and yet it works just as well!

"How's everything?"

One more time, for fun—and for anyone who has ever had to go through the grueling college admissions process. Below is a cartoon originally made funny by Roz Chast and made completely unfunny by me. I took the text and rewrote it to be exactly what you'd expect. There's no surprise to this visual. Nothing funny. And except for the distinctive Roz Chast drawing, you wouldn't really call it a cartoon. In fact, if you saw this in *The New Yorker,* you'd probably wonder what it was doing in there. You might even get angry at the editors for including such an unfunny cartoon. It's a small thing, but you'd feel cheated.

Now here's the actual cartoon. As intended, it works like a cartoon: It's funny.

Why is this funny? Let's think about it. Everything looks pretty familiar—and a lot like the unfunny one created above. The gravestone is the same, except the numbers are different. They're in the same place as above. But rather than the birth year and the death year—as you'd expect—the numbers in the funny cartoon are SAT scores. Why is that funny? SAT scores aren't funny in and of themselves. Neither are gravestones. It's when they're put together that they become funny. No one would ever put their SAT scores on their gravestone. But then, a 720 in math *is* pretty impressive. Hey, why not? Isn't this worth eternal bragging rights? SATs carved in stone! With the unexpected juxtaposition of visual and text, new meaning is created. And it makes us laugh.

Headline Swap: How Print Ads Work

Simple and complex. Synergy with visual and text. Juxtaposition between familiar and fresh. That's what makes a great single-panel cartoon. Sounds like a great print ad, right? So let's see what happens when we take some existing print ads and put them through the same exercise.

Our first example uses an ad from the Absolut Vodka campaign, perhaps the most recognized and well-regarded campaign of the past few decades. As with the cartoon exercise, the first ad, below, is a manipulated version of an existing print ad. The visual is unchanged, but the headline has been revised to read "Absolut Red Tape." In other words, this ad has been purposely changed to make it a "see-say." Since what we're seeing is pretty obvious, the text in this case is especially redundant, flatfooted, and expected. While there are plenty of these types of ads produced, "see-say" has no magic. And neither does the manipulated Absolut ad below. The text doesn't communicate anything to the reader

beyond describing the visual. And because a visual of a bottle wrapped in red tape doesn't say anything about the product, there's no real message about the product or the brand being communicated. In the end, this is just a picture of a bottle wrapped in red tape. We're not quite sure what the modifier "Absolut" has to do with the picture. And we don't particularly care. One thing is for sure: This ad doesn't answer this campaign's strategic objective, which is to communicate perfection . . . absolute perfection.

To the contrary, the original ad below is great. Why? Because the visual and headline are synergistic and unexpectedly meaningful. It invites our brain to combine all the elements together and come up with a greater message: Red Tape + D.C. = An Absolutely Perfect Example of Bureaucracy. To continue with the cartoon analogy, this is the ad's "joke." And like the cartoon, the brain had to work a bit to get there. The text and visual play well with each other. It does what we've come to expect Absolut ads to do: be compelling and imaginative, to make us think for just a second and then have a "moment." Not a chuckle, exactly. But a moment when we realize that we've just witnessed "absolute perfection."

Nice pay off, huh?

Here's another example that works off a Lacoste ad that ran around Christmas season. As before, the first one is modified from the original so that it's flatfooted. It's a clear piece of communication, but it's not very clever and would be easy to overlook in a magazine full of holiday ads.

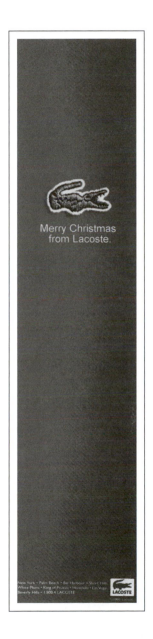

The actual ad is much more engaging. It not only spreads holiday cheer in a clever way but also manages to embed the name of the product in the message. Christmas and Lacoste now become one and the same. It's lively, yet simple. In just a 1/3 column ad, Lacoste manages to grab the readers' attention during the busy holiday season without screaming "I'm a great gift idea."

Because we're having so much fun, let's do one more. This one's from Allstate Insurance on behalf of Mothers Against Drunk Driving (MADD) to dissuade readers from drinking and driving. After being modified for this exercise, the ad becomes a classic "see-say." The visual with the car key in the olive goes a long way toward telling us that this is an ad about mixing alcohol and driving. Unfortunately, the flatfooted headline, "Drinking and driving don't mix," simply repeats that information. Instead of adding something new to the visual, it's rather redundant. Clear but redundant. And that makes the ad a decent piece of communication. But it's not particularly powerful, which is unfortunate because the message really calls out for a punch.

The ad that actually ran makes the point much more compellingly. It works off the same interesting visual but adds a pithy headline, "Killer Cocktail," that really delivers the message. It has a bit of shock value, which this category demands. Unlike the earlier ad, the visual and the headline are not redundant; however, there's no ambiguity about what's being communicated here. So the ad is as clear as the earlier one but also much more provocative. The reader will stay engaged longer, which will increase the chance that the message sinks in.

These AdAnalogies help us understand how a concept works to engage the brain and create a relationship with the reader. When we read an ad or a single-panel cartoon, we're investing a little bit of ourselves. We know that there's a bit of mental work at play. We don't mind, as long as there's a shot that we'll be rewarded in some way. With the cartoon, the reward is a chuckle. A chortle. Or maybe just a grin. Without it, we feel cheated. Or, worse, stupid. Or offended. That's an amazing by-product from a single panel. Usually the reward is pretty fleeting. Once we've had our reaction, we turn the page. But sometimes the cartoon stays with us. We cut it out and tape it to our refrigerator. Or email it to our list of friends.

We should demand that same sort of engagement from advertising, too. The reward is a new way of looking at something or new information that we didn't have before. But if the brain isn't asked to engage from the beginning, then we turn the page or walk away before wasting another moment of our time. As Howard Luck Gossage once said, "People don't read ads, they read what interests them and sometimes it's an ad." That's why conceptual ads work better. They're more interesting. They have a greater chance of grabbing your attention and holding it. That's far superior to ads that are crystal clear and a snooze.

 Visit the student study site at www.sagepub.com/tagstudy for additional online resources including web links, video clips, and recommended readings to learn more about advertising and the creative process.

Critique Exercises

1. At the back of each issue of *The New Yorker* magazine, there's a cartoon caption contest. Participate in the weekly contest—for class purposes or to officially enter! To do this electronically (as well as to vote for current contenders and see a gallery of winners), go to *The New Yorker* website and click on the Caption Contest: http://www .newyorker.com /humor/caption/.

2. On the flip side, take five single-panel cartoons that you think are really funny. Change the caption to make them crystal clear but unfunny.

Suggested Reading

The Naked Cartoonist, by Robert Mankoff, cartoon editor of *The New Yorker*.

Great Collections of Single-Panel Cartoons

The Party After You Left: Collected Cartoons 1995–2003 by Roz Chast

The Unhinged World of Glen Baxter: Volume 1: Collected Works by Glen Baxter

The Far Side Gallery by Gary Larson

The Complete Cartoons of The New Yorker by Robert Mankoff

Chas Addams Happily Ever After: A Collection of Cartoons to Chill the Heart of Your Loved One by Charles Addams

The 360-Degree Critique

Being Digital, Going Viral, and Beyond

In print, "art and copy" play together in mysterious ways. The elements are static, two-dimensional, and discrete. Then the brain comes along and transforms them into something united, dynamic, and meaningful. An advertising concept is not only capable of delivering a strategic message but does so in a memorable and persuasive way. Amazing, eh? Understanding this bit of magic is fundamental to appreciating one of the most powerful ways that advertising communicates. Print is the conceptual bedrock of advertising. It's how Art Directors and Copywriters learn to communicate conceptually, clearly, and cleverly. Regardless of specialty, their portfolio is always filled with print; it's the purest way to demonstrate their creative thinking, discipline, and professional acumen. Print can't hide behind the dimensions of time or space. It doesn't require the sort of collaborative effort that a million-dollar TV commercial does. And despite all the gloom and doom about the demise of magazines and newspapers, print remains a great advertising vehicle. It's not going anywhere. Print advertising is both the training ground and the purest essence of advertising communication. In terms of understanding how this business works, teaching the fundamentals of the process, and learning critique skills, print is still king.

But what about all that other stuff?

Well, the good news is that once you've learned critique basics, you're in pretty good shape to tackle everything else. As I've said, critique is a skill. Once it's mastered in the broad strokes, it's really up to you to hone and apply to the specifics. You should find this truly comforting considering that "all that other stuff," especially social media, interactive advertising, and guerilla, is constantly evolving. It's great to know that the basics will carry you through the next few media revolutions with only slight growing pains. In fact, in such a dynamic marketing environment, critique skills are more valuable than ever. So let's check out the landscape before honing our skills even further.

In the 360-degree world of advertising, anything goes. A major reason for this media fluidity, synergy, and ubiquity is because we live in a digital age. Digital technology has significantly increased communication channels and broken down the boundaries that create discrete silos of advertising communication, such as print and broadcast. Entirely new forms of advertising have come into existence. One of these new forms is broadly called *digital advertising*. But this term can be confusing. On one hand, some types of advertising couldn't exist without digital technology or outside of the digital sphere. On the other hand, digital technology is now used to produce and showcase nearly all forms of traditional advertising. So, to some degree, all media today are digital. Indeed, it won't be long before terms such as *traditional* and *new media* become meaningless as the dividing lines continue to break down. Our terminology is struggling to keep up. And so is our understanding of how everything works together—or if it works at all.

To really confuse things, 360-degree advertising isn't entirely about digitalization. Or the Internet. It's about the way that advertising can now fully embrace us. These days, a strategic message can be delivered in hundreds of different ways and touch nearly all of our senses. So advertising? You're soaking in it.[1]

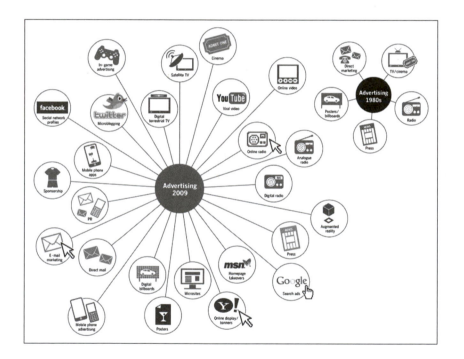

---

[1] "You're soaking in it" is a famous line from an old television campaign for Palmolive liquid soap in which Madge, the manicurist, would prove how mild the dishwashing liquid was by soaking her customers' hands in it. Go to YouTube and type "you're soaking in it" to see one of the spots in this campaign.

Defining Our Media Channels

In order to expand our critique skills, let's first try to define the basic flavors that advertising now comes in.

Print

Enough about print, right? Wrong. We need to define it in the context of 360-degree advertising. Consider print advertising the jumping off point. It's traditionally defined as a two-dimensional message printed on paper. This would include magazine ads, newspaper ads, and billboards. But even from the start, this simple definition hasn't completely held true. Plenty of billboards have their image and text painted on the side of buildings and even barns. No paper. No printing. However, the ads still communicate their message in the same fundamental way: through a two-dimensional combination of image and text. What about static digital ads placed on the Internet, such as banners or simple pop-ups? They're no different than what you'd see in a conventional magazine except that their messages are made possible by using electronic pixels instead of ink. The delivery method is different. The media buy can be more targeted. The call to action mechanism is more immediate. But the way it communicates remains essentially the same. The Internet isn't the only place where print has been transformed. New materials that allow messages to be wrapped around buildings and subway cars are still two-dimensional forms of advertising but no longer flat and opaque. Does this fall into the print category, too? Well, yes. Kinda. Sorta. Unless the ads break free of their self-contained boundaries or become three-dimensional (in which case, they fall into another category of advertising, such as out-of-home, interactive, or experiential), they all fundamentally communicate the same way: two dimensionally. More simply stated, these ads are basically flat with no moving parts. In addition, they stay within hard borders, usually in some dimension of a rectangle. Therefore, let's define this category more by the way it communicates rather than by the material form it takes. Forget ink. Forget paper. In the new world order of 360-degree advertising, this is where we start: static, two-dimensional communication. Print, for short.

Broadcast

Now what's next? Let's stay fairly traditional (although, as I said, we won't be calling it "traditional" for much longer) and add sound plus the dimension of time. In other words, broadcast advertising. This would include television and radio commercials, both in analog and digital formats. However, these are no longer aired exclusively on television sets and radios during specially designated commercial slots during regular programming. Now commercials also air on computer screens. Or gaming consoles. Your cell phone. Billboard monitors. Or in taxi cabs.

This changes things. Once upon a time, the National Association of Broadcasters decided to limit the amount of time in the day that a radio or television station could dedicate to commercial messages. In response to this, programmers limited the length of individual commercials in order to accommodate as many potential advertisers as possible and maximize their revenue. Those lengths have been standardized in order to optimize the designated commercial break. As a consequence, advertisers can't modify the length of their commercials simply to suit their message. Instead, the message has to fit exactly into 60-, 30-, or 15-second units. But commercials aired on new media don't work the same way. When a commercial message appears on the Internet, its length can be dictated more arbitrarily and by many other things: the viewer's attention span, the time it takes to deliver a message, media costs that vary tremendously from website to website. And so on.

Beyond this, radio and television stations must operate in the "public interest," meaning that commercial content is regulated by government agencies. Such scrutiny doesn't necessarily apply to the airing of commercials on user-generated sites such as YouTube. Relieved of such restraints, the signature traits of a commercial are now more broadly defined. But for the purposes of critique, here's the basic definition that we'll use: time-based advertising that delivers its message through words, sound, music (for radio), and visuals in motion. In other words, broadcast advertising.

Hybrids

Then there are the hybrids—the ads that combine elements of static media, broadcast media, and interactivity. A great example of this are the 2009 Apple ads that ran on sites such as *The New York Times*. They have commercial elements such as time, sound, and visuals. They interact with the site itself—as the PC climbs up the side of the page and adjusts *The New York Times* masthead. When the message is over, the elements rest in a traditional print ad position but allow you to both play the ad again or go to the Apple website for greater depth.

Digital

The newest category of advertising is broadly called "digital" and incorporates elements of real life, interactivity, and the digital sphere. It's still developing and often doesn't seem like advertising in the traditional sense. The One Club, the premier organization that promotes excellence in advertising creativity, declared the beginning of the new millennium The Digital Decade.

Their top 10 list includes campaigns such as Burger King's "Subservient Chicken." This

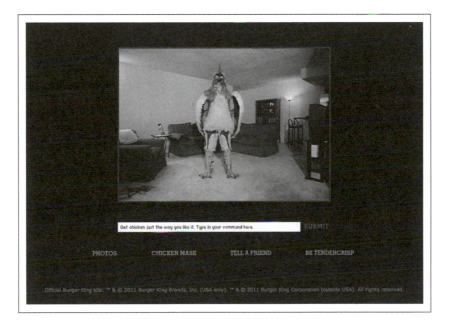

interactive website gave viewers an opportunity to give outrageous commands to a live "chicken" to comedic effect. Developed by Crispin Porter + Bogusky in 2005, this hugely successful effort took their already existing television campaign for Burger King to a new level of consumer engagement, all while supporting their brand message of "having it your way."

Other campaigns on this list include a 2003 BMW digital campaign by Fallon that used mini-films by A-list directors to promote their cars on specially designed websites. Wieden + Kennedy's 2010 "Chalkbot" campaign for Lance Armstrong's LiveStrong Foundation bolted a chalk-spraying printer to the back of a truck that was connected to the Internet. More than 36,000 followers of the Tour de France were able to use SMS technology, social media, and WearYellow.com to text in messages of support and inspiration, which the Chalkbot literally printed onto the actual route of the race.

What's the definition of *digital advertising?* Nick Law, chief creative officer at the premier digital agency, R/GA, calls this category "digital destinations that encourage ongoing engagement" that are integral to—and perhaps even catalysts for—larger campaign plat-forms that consider all channels in 360-degree advertising. In other words, space created on the Web that is discretely dedicated to an advertising message rather than paid media on a sponsor's space. This sort of turns the definition of advertising on it ear. But as the Internet becomes a major channel for delivering content, the rules are being written as we go along. To illustrate this, R/GA created a Nike Plus digital destination that started inside the product itself: Sensors built into Nike + shoes tracked data that were recorded by the runner's iPod. The info was then uploaded onto an interactive site developed by R/GA where athletes could track their progress and connect to a larger community of athletes, thus enabling them to more fully embrace the Nike brand persona. Is this an ad? Or some-thing else entirely? Until we figure out a new way of categorizing this stuff, advertising owns it.

Everything Else—Or That Catchall Category: "Alternative Media"

Now that we've left the world of print, broadcast, and digital, what's left? Everything else. Hence the extremely broad category known as "alternative media." Because dif-ferent forms of media are constantly growing, so is this category. So you might include social media in here if they're an integral part of a broader advertising campaign. Generally speaking, these types of platforms, such as Facebook and Twitter, aren't advertising-friendly because they use two-way communication for brand building and seem more like a public relations vehicle than an advertising one. Unlike agency-generated content, social media is both a controlled and uncontrolled facilitator of information. However, as an ever-growing consumer touch-point, advertising has embraced this outlet as a critical component of brand building and is finding increas-ingly inventive uses for it.

Viral advertising is, like the name suggests, difficult to harness and even harder to manufacture. It's a fairly new term but technically falls into the old-fashioned category of word-of-mouth promotion. As detailed in Malcolm Gladwell's book, *The Tipping Point,* social viruses have long been the genesis for many inexplicable cultural trends. But in the digital age, where user-generated content shares the same platforms as brand-generated messaging, viral advertising turns word-of-mouth into a type of mass communication. This allows viral campaigns to be more visible and powerful than ever. But the potential to be inadvertently destructive is also greater. False steps by an advertiser can be now be quickly and widely exposed to a mass audience. It's also unre-liable: For all the attempts to create a successful viral campaign, only a very few catch on because the tenets of success are elusive—and determined mostly by the whims of the consumer.

Viral advertising uses any number of outlets—both digital and nondigital as well as person-to-person. One well-known Internet platform that turns a consumer inter-est into a form of mass communication is YouTube. An entertaining commercial can be uploaded by a user—either an enthusiastic consumer or the company itself—and then be actively sought after by millions of viewers, giving it a life span well beyond its original intentions. A great example is the 2007 Cadbury commercial featuring a gorilla drumming to the music of Phil Collins. Billboards and magazine ads were created to support the 90-second commercial before it aired in England and Australia. But its real success was achieved when it was placed on YouTube, where it's since been seen by more than 5 million viewers—certainly a surprise success to even the most optimistic at the agency of record, Fallon London. Subsequently, Facebook pages were created to capitalize on the commercial's viral appeal. And the featured song, "In the Air Tonight," shot back onto the charts after its original 1981 success without a physical re-release.

Aside from agency-generated campaigns, even user-generated spoofs of ads can reveal the affection that the public has for a brand. However, the flip side is that bad consumer experiences can be entertaining, too. When documented on cell phones, edited for comedic effect, and then uploaded to sites such as YouTube, such viral experiences can broadside a brand on a mass scale. The Internet's interactive nature gives consumers the opportunity to broadcast their feelings or make fun of ads in ways that were once relegated to personal opinion voiced in the den.

Then there are all types of experiential advertising, such as guerilla (the Cadbury commercial aside, this is spelled "guerilla" and not "gorilla"), events, or ambient forms that all happen in the public sphere. Of course, all advertising is an experience of some sort. But the form of advertising that is called "ambient" or "experiential" distinguishes itself by requiring the consumers' direct participation in a real environment. A good example of this might be the public bathrooms that Charmin built in Times Square in 2005 in order to bring the toilet paper experience directly to consumers.

Sort of experiential, but without any physical interaction with the consumer, is a form of advertising called "out-of-home." Of course, any ad that's experienced beyond the comforts of our house or apartment could technically be referred to as out-of-home. In an era of mobile devices, that would include just about everything. But that's not what this term means. Instead, *out-of-home* refers to ads that break free of print's two-dimensional boundaries and use their context and/or environment to complete their meaning. A great example is the elevator with the Oreo cookie on the side of its car that dunks into a picture of a glass of milk at the bottom of the elevator shaft.

OREO
Milk's favorite cookie.   The traditional dunk of an Oreo cookie into a glass of milk was dramatized with the use of a panoramic elevator in a shopping mall. This attention-grabbing use of new media gave us one more way to show that Oreo is milk's favorite cookie.

Another great example to illustrate how "out-of-home" works is this poster for peace. As flat artwork, it looks like a traditional print ad, but its message isn't complete until it is wrapped around a pole. In other words, the environment helps to complete the message: "What goes around, comes around."

Marshall McLuhan once stated, "The medium is the message." Few industries have appreciated this more than advertising. The physical form of an ad, the media buy, and the context in which it is experienced have always been integral to a message's effectiveness. With today's media ubiquity, this is especially true. But in another sense, the onus has never been higher on the message and campaign concept to be its own differentiator. This elevates the importance of critique on many levels. Critique helps determine whether a message is being appropriately amplified by its chosen media channel. In addition, deconstructing advertising in order to determine whether all the parts communicate as a powerful whole is fundamental to evaluating any sort of advertising—whether it's a simple print ad or full-blown multimedia campaign.

Timeline and Traits of Media Channels

Here's my timeline that also distinguished the characteristics unique to each form—and which any advertiser must appreciate in order to make the most of their chosen media channels. It's important to note that new technology doesn't replace old technology; it just adds onto it. The more we create, the more important it becomes to coordinate and synergize the various media that any campaign uses (hence the new popularity of Project Managers at agencies).

PRINT ▶ **RADIO**

Print: static and two-dimensional (i.e., magazine and newspaper ads and billboards)

Radio: subtracts visuals; adds time and sound

TELEVISION ▶ ALTERNATIVE MEDIA

Television: adds visuals to time and sound

Alternative media: static, three-dimensional, and the environment must give meaning to the concept

DIGITAL HYBRIDS ▶ DIGITAL

Digital hybrids: uses any combined characteristics of traditional media that allow it to exist as paid space on Internet sites

Digital: lives discretely (not embedded in another communication vehicle such as a magazine, newspaper, or television show), adds interactivity and has more latitude with time and space

SOCIAL MEDIA

Social media: adds consumer voice
as part of the messaging

AdSpeak 360

So now that we have a basic understanding of all the media forms that advertising can take, let's look at a few multimedia campaigns and apply our critique skills using AdSpeak.

In Chapter 2, we defined an advertising campaign as multiple ads anchored in a single concept. This is true regardless of whether the ads take the form of print, broadcast, digital, or alternative media. This is also true when the media are mixed as in a multimedia campaign. The definition of a concept, however, is broader when applied to a multimedia campaign than it is when defining a print concept. That's because print communicates in a very focused, two-dimensional way in which art and copy work synergistically to create meaning. But broadcast adds time and sound. Out-of-door adds a third dimension. Digital adds interactivity. A single concept still anchors such disparate elements of a multimedia effort to create a campaign, but in order to accommodate media forms that communicate in different ways, the concept needs to be more elastic. So we have to loosen up the definition a bit. In a multimedia campaign, the concept is more broadly defined as the big idea that unites all campaign elements.

Case Study: The California Milk Processor Board's "Got Milk?" From Print to Television to Out-of-Home/Experiential

Let's revisit the "got milk?" print campaign and then examine how it attaches itself to the bigger multimedia campaign. First, we have to back up to the strategy. Or the WHAT. What did this campaign want us to know? That milk is uniquely satisfying; indeed, when it's paired with certain foods, nothing else will do. The print delivered this message with its concept (or the HOW) of featuring those foods with a big bite taken out—making you, the consumer, feel as though you've got a big mouthful. But what's missing? The milk. Suddenly, you've never quite realized how much you want a glass of milk. In even simpler terms, the concept is the dramatization of the absence of milk by featuring a yummy food. In this way, the strategic message is delivered to your head and in your gut.

Here's one of the print executions in this campaign. It shows a close-up of the food against seamless. The food is the star, and the big bite is the focus. To draw extra attention to it, the tagline asks the question that's on the tip of your taste buds: Got milk?

The print campaign was part of a larger multimedia campaign produced by the agency Goodby, Silverstein & Partners. As you'll see, the concept is the same no matter what the media: dramatizing the absence of milk through the presence of a yummy food. By remaining anchored in the same concept, all the ads—no matter what form they take—become part of a larger, singularly focused communications campaign rather then individual ads. Staying nonspecific in our articulation of the concept allows us to add other media forms into the mix.

Here's the first commercial done in the "got milk?" campaign. This 1993 award-winning spot features a history buff surrounded by obscure Aaron Burr memorabilia and enjoying a peanut butter sandwich. As he puts the last big bite into his mouth, a radio announcer telephones with a trivia question: For $10,000, does he know the name of the person who shot Alexander Hamilton? Unfortunately, with a mouthful of peanut butter and no milk,

:30 "Aaron Burr" Got Milk TV Commercial

the best answer he can give is "Awoon Buur," and he misses the opportunity of a lifetime. This spot went on to become one of the most memorable of all time, placing 11th on *Entertainment Weekly*'s 1998 list of "50 Greatest Commercials of All Time."

The concept behind this spot adheres to the larger campaign concept: A yummy food is featured to dramatize the absence of milk. In this way, it fits alongside the print campaign as part of the larger "got milk?" campaign. However, the execution of the television commercial is different from the print execution. This spot does not treat the food as a large, iconic visual against seamless. Instead, this execution works better with the medium in which it is delivered: broadcast. Now that the advertiser has the luxury of time, sound, and acting, the concept is now executed as a mini-movie. There's drama and exaggerated humor. There's a buildup of plot and climax of action. The lighting is cinematic. There's a musical score to accentuate the action. Despite the fact that the television campaign and the print campaign don't look exactly alike, they are clearly part of a larger campaign because they are anchored in the same concept.

As with print campaigns, each commercial in a TV campaign is not only an outgrowth of a single concept but also has a similar executional style. Each spot has a similar setup but a different scenario. It's not necessary to always use the same director, but keeping the same visual style helps make the campaign more unified and easily recognizable. And as we've learned from AdSpeak, that's much more powerful than airing a series of random spots. So let's see this in action with two other "got milk?" spots.

The award-winning 2003 spot, "Birthday," is reminiscent of the horror film, *The Omen,* and features a young boy who can predict when bad things are about to happen. To set up the premise, the child, who's being driven to a birthday party, obliquely tells the driver to stop. When the car screeches to a halt, it narrowly avoids hitting a dog. In the next scene, the boy and his companion are walking outside toward the party; the boy obliquely says "stop" and his companion obeys. Suddenly, a tree crashes down in front of them, missing them by inches. At the party, as guests are about to dig into the birthday cake, the child once again utters the word *stop.* The children ignore him and eat the cake. When everyone's mouths are full, the hostess runs out from the kitchen in a panic to announce that she's out of milk. The guests suddenly appreciate the horror of the situation the freaky clairvoyant child had foreseen.

:30 "Birthday" Got Milk TV Commercial

As in the Aaron Burr spot, this commercial establishes a plot line that allows the story to come to a climax in a mere 30 seconds. That climax, of course, happens after the characters' mouths are filled with a yummy food and there's the realization that there's no milk to wash it down. The message is delivered at the moment of desire, because that's when it's most viscerally appreciated. One could equate the climax in these spots to that bite in the print ads. In the layout, the tagline "got milk?" is purposely placed near the empty bite, which accentuates that moment of desire. Similarly, the "got milk?" tagline in the commercial comes a beat after the moment of realization.

The third spot, produced in 1995, uses a classic detective interrogation scene to drive home the strategic message that there's nothing worse than not having milk. As two detectives attempt to get a jailbird to sing, they offer him a cupcake, which he greedily crams into his mouth. When his mouth is full, they push a milk carton slightly out of reach. Just before cutting to the tagline, "got milk?" we cut to close-up of the criminal, cheeks full with chocolate all over his face, looking totally despondent and aware that he's just been duped. Same concept as the earlier spots? Yes, the absence of milk as appreciated in the most visceral way: with a mouthful of yummy food. Same concept as the print campaign? Yes, ditto. New scenario, but same executional style as the earlier spots? Yes, again. Same execution as the print ads? Not exactly, but certainly within the more elastic framework of a multimedia campaign.

:30 "Interrogation" Got Milk TV Commercial

Now let's add another media channel to the mix. In this case, out-of-home. Using the traditional media space of a bus shelter, the ad below used the poster space to put nothing more than the tagline. It turned into out-of home when the agency played with the environment and added another dimension: the dimension of smell (is this a dimension? I guess so). Billed as the first ad campaign to have an olfactory component to it, this ad sprayed the aroma of chocolate chip cookies in the air. The campaign concept is clearly delivered: a yummy food (albeit the smell of it) without milk (as accentuated by the "got milk?" tagline in plain sight). Of course, the execution is different than either the television commercials or the print ads. In true out-of-home style, this ad works with its environment to bring the idea to life. And because the campaign idea is so clearly delivered, consumers completely accept this as another ad in the "got milk?" campaign. We already know that the concept is strategic. So is this execution doing a good job of delivering the message to consumers? As it turns out, not really. While the press loved the idea and helped create a lot of buzz around this execution, the people waiting at the bus stop hated it. The cookie smell made them nauseous. And no one wants milk when they're nauseous. So in this example, we have a great delivery on concept, but the execution ended up undermining the strategic message.

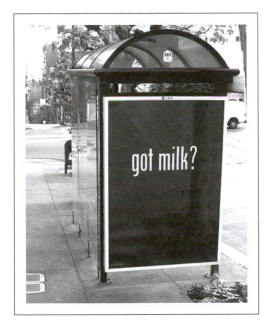

Katy Raddatz / The Chronicle

The "got milk?" campaign has been incredibly successful. The print was powerful, but the synergistic uses of other media amplified the message and raised the level of awareness dramatically. Over the years, the "got milk?" campaign has not only won nearly every advertising award in the book, including One Show and Canne awards, but in 1995 it won a Gold Effie, a national honor awarded to advertisers who have achieved their marketing objectives. In 2005, Taglineguru.com named "got milk?" as the "most culturally influential tagline since the advent of broadcast television" (http://www.gotmilk.com/#/gotmilkbrand/brand-history/). Finally and most important, after years of declining milk consumption, people were drinking more milk only months after this campaign began.

Case Study: Dove's "Real Beauty" Campaign: From Print to Television to Viral to Digital to Social Media

Unilever's 2004 global study on women's attitudes toward beauty resulted in a key insight: Women did not feel that they measured up to the media's unrealistic representations of the female ideal and consequently did not define themselves as beautiful. This led them, along with their ad agency, Ogilvy & Mather, to create the "Real Beauty" campaign for the Unilever brand, Dove. Its strategic message resonated so strongly with women across the country that it's considered one of the most successful and meaningful campaigns of the millennium's first decade. The target for this campaign was broadly aimed at all women of all shapes and sizes. Of course, if men got the point, too, that would be great—but more for society than the brand itself since Dove's personal care products are predominantly made for women. The age span of the target, from senior citizens to young girls, is quite wide. However, the message was to build up brand image by building up the self-esteem of women in the general population. Indeed, it wages a

battle between "us" and "them"—all those unnaturally skinny models that only exist on the runways in Paris and Milan. The scope of the campaign made it ripe for multimedia so its message could find a channel that spoke to some facet in their wide demographic.

The campaign concept is straightforward: to visualize the truth and celebrate the beauty of ordinary women who would normally not find their way into advertising. In print, this concept is executed using simple portraits of women shot by Annie Leibovitz against white seamless with headlines that challenge the readers to redefine beauty based on what they were seeing. The portraits look clean—which makes sense for a soap company. They have a straightforward honesty about them (but see the first Critique Exercise at the end of this chapter). This helps deliver the message of real beauty. There's no mood lighting or exotic environment to either detract or enhance the women on the page. The women stand on their own. Looking directly into the camera, they appear unashamed of themselves or of being looked at. Staring back at the page, the reader bonds with models and their message in an almost conspiratorial way. Synergistic billboards and television commercials, all with regular people against seamless, ran concurrently with the print.

One interesting amplification of the "Real Beauty" campaign was a 75-second video created by Ogilvy & Mather Toronto that aired initially and primarily on YouTube. It did not share the clean executional look of the print or television ads. Instead, it felt like a documentary exposing some hidden truth about media deception. Called "Evolution," it shows the transformation of a regular woman into a glamorous model through makeup,

lighting, and the magic of retouching. While stylistically different than the more slickly produced advertising, it a part of the larger campaign because it is anchored in the same "Real Beauty" concept that visualizes the truth and celebrates the beauty of ordinary women. What makes this a smart addition to the campaign is how well it understands and works with its viral medium in order to deliver the same campaign message. While it's essentially the same message, in this platform it feels edgier, more subversive, like an expose. In part, this is because there's no overt selling. No products are featured or even mentioned. The footage looks a bit raw as though someone shot it on the sly. All of these executional aspects help authenticate the film, which, in turn, help authenticate the more commercial elements of the "Real Beauty" campaign. Slightly longer than a traditional commercial and giving off a "we don't play by the rules" vibe, it feels at home on a site such as YouTube where most clips are user generated. Still, this film doesn't hide the fact that it's sponsored by a company. While there are no products in sight, the film opens with a roughly written title, "a Dove film." It ends with an invitation to help the Dove Self Esteem Fund. This commercial association hasn't stopped the film from going viral. Over 1 million people have watched it on YouTube. Appreciating its power, Unilever has also

aired versions of this on television and in cinemas in the Netherlands and the Middle East. Its greatest power, however, come from user-generated interest on the Internet.

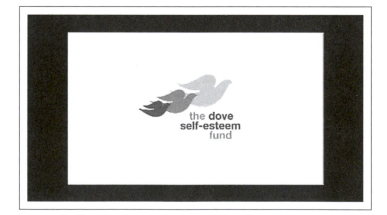

To make good on its commitment to "Real Beauty," Unilever established the Dove Self Esteem Fund and created a website dedicated to mother-daughter workshops, parental advice, a "self-esteem zone" for young girls, and other interactive features on behalf of the campaign for "Real Beauty." The site includes the original global study by Unilever, which found that "only 2% of women around the world identify themselves as beautiful" (http://www.dove.us /#/ CFRB/arti_CFRB.aspx[cp-documentid = 7049726]). There are also links to other women's authorities such as Girls Scouts and Girls, Inc. These concrete details not only create a richer experience on the site but also validate Dove's campaign. Beyond servicing the brand, this is a digital platform for a real cause that Dove helped to identify and promote. In turn, this enhances Dove's image as a beauty company that deeply cares about real women and their issues.

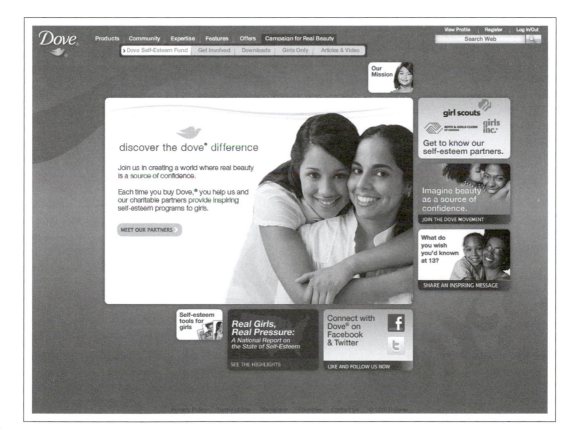

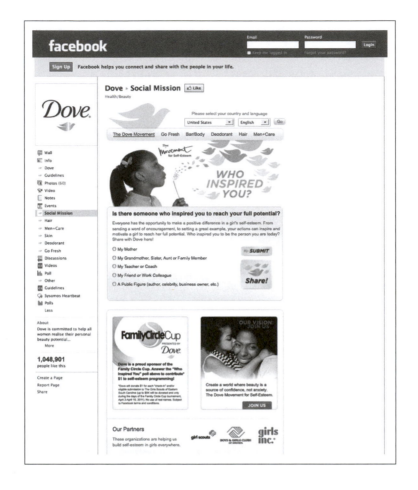

Adding social media to the mix, Dove created a Facebook page for the "Real Beauty" campaign that allowed consumers not only to have a two-way dialogue about their products but also to discuss self-esteem issues for young women. While faithful to the mediums in which they exist, all the different forms of advertising tied themselves to the larger "Real Beauty" campaign through message consistency, use of language and tone, honest visuals, and clean graphics.

This 360-degree approach helps make this campaign less of a promotional effort than a social mission. In a world in which we value companies that embody our own ethics, the "Real Beauty" campaign can claim two benefits: better self-esteem for women and an increase in sales. This campaign also makes good on Ogilvy & Mather's principles of the 4Es: Experience, Everyplace, Exchange, and Evangelism—which are at the heart of 360-degree advertising.

Case Study: Old Spice's "Smell Like a Man, Man": TV to Social Media to Print

Few campaigns have captured the public's attention as swiftly as the 2010 Old Spice "Smell Like a Man, Man," campaign. It seemed to come out of nowhere. Despite practically inventing the body wash category for men, Old Spice hadn't been advertising for years and was relying on established name recognition. Based on new research, its ad agency, Weiden + Kennedy, found that with competition flooding the market, Old Spice had lost its distinction. In addition, because women are often the main purchasers of this product, they'd buy whatever body wash worked for everyone. According to Weiden + Kennedy's case study on this campaign (creativity-online.com/work/old-spice...case-study/20896), their strategy was to emphasize Old Spice's manly scent and to disparage the more perfume-y body washes on the market. Their research convinced the company to target both men and women.

So what concept did Weiden + Kennedy come up with to deliver that strategic message? They invented a living embodiment of "the man your man could smell like." In other words, an exaggerated "spokesguy" (played by actor Isaiah Mustafa) who epitomizes every cliché that a woman could ever want in a guy, all made possible by using Old Spice. Executionally, these spots show our incredibly fit and dashingly handsome spokesguy speaking directly to camera, addressing the ladies in the audience, and demonstrating extreme examples of his manliness. The style is exaggerated, stylized, and even a bit cheesy. The tone of the spokesguy is over-the-top confident, seductive, and macho—the real authority. While speaking to directly "the ladies," the spot's intended to appeal to both men and women. In fact, Weiden + Kennedy hoped to spark conversation among couples. And these commercials do. Aside from simply being funny, they're provocative. Men start to wonder if their body wash IS too perfume-y to be manly. And women begin to think about buying Old Spice for their significant others. As provocative as they are, they're also transparent: These ads overtly sell the product in classic pitchman style. Indeed, the spokesguy is so beloved that the viewer becomes grateful to Old Spice for delivering him to us. Almost a parody, but not quite, the commercials seem to wink at the viewers, who know they're being sold to, but don't mind at all.

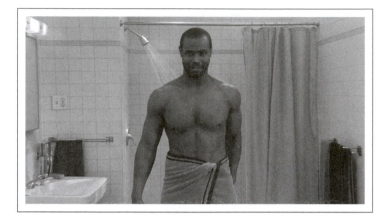

Script from the original 30-second commercial

Spokesguy speaking directly to camera:

Hello, ladies.

Look at your man.

Now back to me.

Now back at your man.

Now back to me.

Sadly, he isn't me.

But if he stopped using lady scented body wash

and switched to Old Spice,

he could smell like he's me.

Look down.

Back up.

Where are you?

You're on a boat

with the man your man could smell like.

What's in your hand?

Back at me.

I have it.

It's an oyster with two tickets to that thing you love.

Look again.

The tickets are now diamonds.

Anything is possible

when your man smells like Old Spice

and not a lady.

I'm on a horse.

Launched online during Super Bowl weekend in 2010 and then broadcast on TV, this 30-second spot was an immediate hit with consumers (and then the award shows). The original ad has been seen by over tens of millions of YouTube users. Sales for Old Spice soared and ultimately put Old Spice back on top. All because of a 30-second commercial—the advertising form often rumored to be on its way out. Why? Good strategy. Smart concept. Great writing, casting, and acting. Consumers bonded with the spokesguy and looked forward to what he'd say next. Indeed, part of the appeal of the commercial is that you want to see it again and again. It's funny, even after multiple viewings. More commercials were produced. The buzz grew.

Appreciating the relationship that the Old Spice guy was developing with consumers, Weiden + Kennedy looked to expand the campaign using media channels that would allow the spokesguy to speak more directly to his audience. Social media seemed obvious, but Weiden + Kennedy wanted to harness this medium more appropriately and innovatively for the purposes of the "Smell Like a Man, Man" campaign. Rather than simply create Twitter or Facebook platforms that usually subjugate the advertising concept in favor of two-way, less controlled consumer-driven communication, the social media aspects of the Old Spice campaign gave consumers a degree of control but only in ways that adhered to the campaign concept. First, the agency created an Old Spice YouTube channel where versions of the popular commercials could air anytime consumers wanted to see them. Then Old Spice provided an engagement opportunity by asking consumers to submit direct questions via Twitter and Facebook to the Old Spice spokesguy. After acquiring three days worth of questions, the agency filmed the Old Spice spokesguy directly answering over 183 of them with personalizing details, including the names of those asking the questions. He remained in character, offering up quirky advice and reminding viewers to "Smell Like a Man, Man" by using Old Spice. Then they broadcast those answers on YouTube.

According to Jack Marshal in a July 2010 article in *ClickZ,* the social media aspect of this campaign attracted over 35 million individual views in just seven days. The final video reply compelled over 5,800 people to post comments within hours. In just seven days after it launched, "total upload views for the channel, a metric that includes the original TV ads, [stood] at over 92 million." Within days, the brand's official Twitter account had over 32,000 followers. By any measure, the social media aspects of this campaign, building on the overall campaign concept of "Smell Like a Man, Man," were an enormous success.

Building even further on this campaign's success, Weiden + Kennedy decided to go completely old school and add print to the media mix. Bound by its two dimensionality, the print concept connects to the television spots but adjusts for the medium. Here, the Old Spice spokesguy, still played by Isaiah Mustafah, embodies all of his manliness in a single still image. The concept turns the spokesguy into a literal landing point for all things manly and wonderful. In this way, he is literally the "freshest place on earth." The print concept is true to its form yet still clearly adheres to both the larger campaign message and strategy. In addition to running in men's magazines (the ad below was last spotted in a *Sports Illustrated* issue dated February 2011), these ads were used on the Internet and as design elements on Facebook and The Old Spice YouTube channel. Being synergistic with all elements of the campaign enables Old Spice to speak to consumers in a more immersive 360-degree way.

It's a 360-Degree World: Respect Your Media

The basic rules for 360-degree campaigns are to remain true to the campaign concept while also using each media channel in terms of how it works best. Make sure each expression of the campaign has value. Or don't do it. Understand the power of each media form and use it accordingly. Never lose sight of your strategy. And respect the power of your campaign concept. It can be pretty elastic. But don't stretch it so far that it snaps. Don't use media "just because" they're sexy, new, or cheaper. Grant McCracken, author of Chief Culture Officer and research affiliate at C3 in MIT, holds that traditional

	SENDER (advertiser)	MEDIUM	AUDIENCE (consumer)	LITERACY REQUIREMENTS
Salesmanship	Seller (who may also be maker)	Interpersonal	One, or a few	None
Salesmanship in Print	Client + Agency	Mass	Many, all at once	Literacy
Broadcasting Radio	Client + Agency	Mass	Many, all at once	None
Broadcasting TV (radio w/pictures)	Client + Agency	Mass	Many, all at once	None
Narrowcasting a) Cable b) Videotape	Client + Agency Client + Agency	Mass Mass	Fragmented and able to shift viewing time	Technological literacy
Internet, etc.	Client + Agency + CONSUMER!	Personalized	Atomized	Computer and Internet literacy

advertising has a unique way of delivering a message that is sometimes undervalued in a climate where there are so many "sexy" media channels to pick from. At the 2011 ARF Re:Think Conference, he pointed to a number of companies who abandoned television in favor of social media, hoping to increase the buzz around their brand and instead ended up losing a seat at the table to brands that continued their presence on TV.

Examples such as "got milk?" for the California Milk Processor Board, "Real Beauty" for Dove, and "Smell Like a Man, Man" for Old Spice show how the power of campaigns can be amplified by the proper and collaborative use of media. Old Spice started its campaign traditionally with a strong concept that was masterfully executed as 30-second TV commercials. The spots were then placed in nonpaid media channels to create a viral effect. The campaign—still anchored firmly in the same concept—was expanded to include social media in an interactive way that maintained the integrity of the campaign concept. Finally, Old Spice added the most traditional form of media of all—print ads—to reinforce the relationship it had so wonderfully cultivated with consumers. That's 360-degree advertising at its best.

 Visit the student study site at www.sagepub.com/tagstudy for additional online resources including web links, video clips, and recommended readings to learn more about advertising and the creative process.

Critique Exercises

1. In 2005, a story came out about all the retouching that many of the Dove ads required before they made it to publication. Normally, this wouldn't make headlines. But in this case, it undermined the power of the concept. Explain why.

2. Find a campaign that started out in a single medium and branched out to include others. How well does each medium work? Was the concept elastic enough to embrace other forms of media? Was the message strengthened or weakened by the addition of new media?

3. Take one of your own print campaign concepts and extend it to three more media channels, for example, radio, television, out-of-home, and social media. Stay true to the concept, but also take full advantage of each medium's characteristics.

4. Go to the OBIE Awards (from the OAAA). See the gallery at either http://www .oaaa.org/awards/obieawards.aspx or www.aef.com/exhibits/awards/obie_awards. Identify the difference between a traditional billboard and an experiential ad. Critique: WHAT. WHO. HOW. WHERE.

5. Become a flâneur and stumble across five examples of alternative media (do NOT use Google or design/advertising annuals, collections, etc.). Take a picture. Critique: WHAT. WHO. HOW. WHERE.

Find Out More

- Read the case study on "got milk?" in the AEF case history section: http://www.aef .com/on_campus/classroom/case_histories/landing

- Read more about the Old Spice campaign in William M. O'Barr (2011). "Creativity in Advertising," *Advertising & Society Review, 11*(4), E-ISSN: 1534-7311 on Project Muse (http://muse.jhu.edu/journals/advertising_and_society_review/v011/11.4.o-barr01.html).

- Read the article on the Dove "Real Beauty" campaign in the "Dove Campaign Roundtable" (2008), *Advertising & Society Review, 9*(4), E-ISSN: 1534-7311 on Project Muse (http://muse.jhu.edu/journals/advertising_and_society_review/v009/9.4.fielding.html).

Critique in Action

CHAPTER 6

AdAlliances

Your Partners in Creating Great Advertising

The Dance

The ultimate goal of *Ad Critique* is to help create a more collaborative and productive work environment where the creative product is not just respected but understood. Where agency executives and brand managers not only look forward to meetings with creative professionals but engage in meaningful dialogue. To achieve this goal, the first half of the book identified critique as a misunderstood but essential skill set for everyone and offered up lessons on acquiring those skills. So now you're an expert, right? Not so fast. Before applying your newfound knowledge, you need to get a better feeling for the process and the participants. A successful critique is like an intuitive dance. It's a tricky activity that's driven by uniquely talented yet collaborative individuals. So don't take to the dance floor until you know your partner. And practice your moves.

Of course, this lovely dance metaphor makes critique sound like an inherently friendly process. It should be. But as discussed much earlier in the book, it is often treated as an adversarial exercise. Understandable. Prima facie, critique seems like a destructive act rather than a constructive process that makes the work better. On top of this, advertising encourages and even glorifies the "creative/management" divide. So the players involved in critique may seem less like dance partners and more like nasty, blood-thirsty opponents at opposite ends of the field. Therefore, the next few chapters are dedicated to understanding why this is and how we can harness our differences, mesh our strengths, tame our egos, and be better partners in order to accomplish our mutual goals: great advertising.

The Cast of Characters

Great advertising is the product of many people. However, there are a few major players who truly drive the process. In order to strengthen our alliances, let's start by identifying who we're talking about.

The Brand Team, AKA "The Client": played by a bunch of folks in the marketing department of a company who represent and manage the brand. Chances are, they hold MBAs. They're marketing mavens who are well versed in the 4Ps: product, promotion, placement, and place. The number of people on this team depends on the size of the company. At a place like Procter & Gamble, there are many players on a team (supervisors, managers, assistant managers, etc.) for a single product. At really small companies that don't even have a department dedicated to marketing, the Brand Team may be the Mom & Pop who run the shop. Whatever the case, these are the people who the agency is generally speaking about when you hear the term "The Client" because they're the people who most directly interface with the agency.

The Account Team: played by the bunch of advertising people who act as the liaison between the client and the rest of the agency. In a large agency, it takes a large number of people to manage a single account. They are responsible for analyzing marketing problems for the client and coming up with advertising solutions. Account Executives (AEs), Assistant AEs, and Account Supervisors are in the unique position of having to transmit both the agency's recommendations to the client and the client's interests to the Creatives. In this regard, they are on the front lines of critique. In small agencies, Account Managers are the main developers of the creative strategy; in larger agencies, this responsibility often falls on Strategic Planners, who work closely with Account Managers, Market Researchers, and Creatives in order to produce more insightful, consumer-driven strategies.

The Creative Director: played by someone who has risen from the ranks of either Copywriter or Art Director. The Creative Director oversees the process rather than participates in it. If the Creative Department is large, there may be other levels of oversight. Titles might include Group Creative Director, Associate Creative Director, or whatever happening nomenclature the agency chooses. Because the Creative Director is considered part of management, he or she is also involved in aspects of strategic development.

The Creative Team: In the idea industry, the key manufacturers of these ideas are not part of an assembly line, but a fairly unique pairing of individuals played by the Art Director and Copywriter—one team per campaign. Unlike the account team of a large agency, they usually work on more than one account at a time. Together, they're seen as a single unit and are often more simply called "the Team" or "the Creatives."

But wait a minute. Isn't everyone who works in advertising "creative"? Yes, they are. Everyone in every department is expected to come up with creative solutions—even if they work in the mailroom. Media planning requires creativity. Strategic development requires creativity. Dealing with the client requires creativity. Assessing the work requires creativity (or at least killer critique skills!). However, not everyone gets to work in a department called "creative." So who are these "idea makers" with the audacious title? Here are some of the basics:

* The team approach to advertising is an innovation of Bill Bernbach (of Doyle Dane Bernbach, now DDB Worldwide. Remember him? He is a god to me).

- Creatives are teamed because, like a good ad, the aspects of art and copy are intricately, yet seamlessly intertwined. Indeed, the line between the two jobs is often blurred.

- Both deal with the principal aspects of the ad—the concept, the headline, the execution. More senior teams are involved in some aspects of strategic development.

- In addition to being artistic and trained in the finer points of their discipline, they must be strong communicators, intuitive, persuasive, and daring.

- Art Directors are more responsible for the layout and design sensibilities of an ad. They must be proficient in design software; however, the actual design and implementation of an ad are handed over to studio designers but overseen by the Art Director. The Copywriter is more involved in the nitty-gritty of the copy. That means when a commercial requires dialogue, the Copywriter is instrumental in directing the talent.

Knee-Jerk Reactions to Those on the Other Side of the Table

Now that we've got the major players down, let's figure out the dynamics that are counterproductive to the process and lead to the creative/management divide. Remember the 1985 campaign developed by Fallon McElligott Rice for *Rolling Stone* magazine called "Perception/Reality"? At the time, the magazine was losing media dollars because advertisers perceived the readership to comprise aging hippies. The reality was starkly different: Most readers were fairly youthful with a moderately high income and education level. The concept of this campaign was to visualize that discrepancy. It was a powerful device that successfully got the attention of media buyers. Armed with the truth, ad revenue increased over 80% in a few short years.

This is our truth, too. And perhaps this truth will set us free: Our perceptions of each other do not completely align with reality. Of course, the Creatives do associate themselves with the more creative aspects of the business, and management does tend to associate itself with the more business-like aspects of marketing and ad management. And that creates a polarization of interests. Which is good, to a point; we all have our own jobs to do. As any psychologist will tell us, feeling distinctly talented makes us feel better about ourselves. Unique. And more important. Creatives, especially, perform better when they think of themselves as "the other." So there's a reason to cultivate this divide. But there's also a downside. We may decide that our weaknesses are not something to overcome, but something used to accentuate our strengths. We put on "personas." We buy into the "us versus them" mind-set. We become content in the belief that MBAs don't quite mix with the MFAs. It's easier to assume that "they wear suits, so their numbers must be right" or "they have ponytails, so their work must be creative." We become way too comfortable with these assumptions. It is what it is. And all's right with the world. Right?

Wrong. Snap out of it. The folks on the creative divide need to shake some of their knee-jerk thinking. Ditto those on the management team. Epiphany alert: A smart businessperson IS a creative person. He or she may not be able to draw a still life or compose a novella, but success in the marketplace requires innovation, and innovation requires creativity. Business folk need to embrace that part of their personality, use it to better understand critique, and channel it during the collaborative process.

Conversely: A smart advertising creative IS business-minded. He or she is not creating ads to hang on the living room wall or make the best-seller list but in order to sell a product. The vehicle for this sort of salesmanship happens to be creativity. It is a means to an end—not the end in and of itself. The creative team in an advertising agency is the ultimate problem solver, not only helping to develop strategies but creating solutions that make an impact and compel consumers to act. That's creativity and salesmanship all rolled up into one. So there's no excuse for them not to call upon such business-minded traits when dealing with those on the other side of the aisle.

Such characterizations may be liberating, but they won't flush years of knee-jerk thinking out of your system. Successful critique begins with an outstretched hand. So we all need to try harder. Here's an exercise that might help. Let's get all those stereotypical thoughts out on the table and examine them to see how much water they hold. Let it all hang out. Consider every petty thought that ever existed in your head that defines a client. Or account guy. Or Art Director. This way, you can really see your perceptions for what they are. Kinda true, like most stereotypes. But really kinda not.

In 60 seconds or less, write down the five adjectives that you think best describe a Copywriter.

1.

2.

3.

4.

5.

In 60 seconds or less, write down the five adjectives that you think best describe an Art Director.

1.

2.

3.

4.

5.

In 60 seconds or less, write down the five adjectives that you think best describe an agency account executive.

1.

2.

3.

4.

5.

In 60 seconds or less, write down the five adjectives that you think best describe a brand manager or the client who oversees the advertising.

1.

2.

3.

4.

5.

The responses to the above will depend a lot on which side of the aisle you see yourself on. For example, if you're on the business side, you might describe an agency account person as "buttoned up," whereas the same trait might be interpreted as "anal" by someone who sits on the creative side of the aisle. This is partly the point of the exercise: We all come to it with our set of biases, and this should make them more clear to us. Now give yourself a moment to review what you've written. Do you see a pattern? If the five adjectives in each category were put together and turned into an ice cream, would the Creatives come across like Ben & Jerry's flavor of the month? And would the business folk seem more like vanilla fudge? Furthermore, consider how accurate your assessments are. How much knee-jerk thinking went into your profiles?

Stories From the Combat Zone

First, let's concede that there's nothing wrong with either of those flavors, even if they're not your personal favorites. Vanilla's great and versatile. Pistachio chocolate chunk is mighty tasty, too. We can celebrate the deliciousness of both. Second, let's try to expand the ways in which we define each other—no matter which category you fit under. Here is some anecdotal evidence that might get you beyond the stereotypes.

Story Number One. A former Art Director partner of mine was constantly frustrated by clients who didn't fully appreciate his artistic vision. He'd create these clever ads. The client wouldn't bite. If he had been brutally honest with himself, he'd admit that he sometimes had issues with sticking to the strategy. But he wasn't inclined to give the client an inch. At meetings, they'd always lock horns. After a while, they couldn't stand to look at each other anymore. My sense was that, for the most part, the client was not taking issues with his creativity but with the nonstrategic aspects of the work. But neither of them was able to articulate (through critique!) what was truly at issue. So they both stewed. A lot. Finally, my partner left advertising altogether and went into a different line of business: He started to design ties. Beautiful ties made from Italian silk and conceived around cleaver motifs. He's not only the key designer, but he owns the company. He built it from scratch. He's now a great success (check out his ties at www.joshbach.com). To me, this proves that he actually did possess plenty of business acumen. But back in the advertising world, this was not entirely apparent. The skill was dormant; the muscle was undeveloped—possibly because it was never meant to be. Since his ties are terrific and his business is a great success, this story has a happy ending. However, for those of you without a back-up plan, learning how to critique early on could really empower your career.

Story Number Two. A president from a large advertising agency, who had come up from the management side of the business, loved to wear denim shirts and blue jeans to important meetings. He felt that this not only showed off his "creative side" but might confuse people into thinking he was a member of the creative department. Of course, no one really confused him with the Art Director or Copywriter because they all knew he was president of the agency. But everyone always feigned confusion because they wanted to stroke his ego. Why not? He was the president. One day, both members of his top creative team showed up at a meeting in really, really nice suits. The president, of course, was wearing his usual denim shirt. Despite the fact that the Creatives were in the suits, the client had no problem identifying them as the Art Director and Copywriter of the business. Their work was great. The client respected them. All questions were aimed at them. Not at the suits, but the people inside them. In the meantime, no one talked to the guy in the denim shirt. The president was not pleased. In fact, even though the client was happy, he was pissed. After the meeting, he teased the team about their suits and suggested that they dress down for the next presentation. They didn't. They wore really, really nice suits. He teased them again, only this time, it seemed like more of a threat than a tease. But to show the president who wore the real creative pants in the agency, they refused to wear denim shirts. They were renegades. They knew it was the work that mattered, not how funky their clothing was. So they kept wearing really, really nice suits. They started wearing them to minor meetings without the client. Pretty soon, they were wearing nice suits every day of the week. A few months later, they were fired. See how perverse some of these perceptions can get?

Story Number Three. There are even stereotypes within stereotypes. For example, some believe that Copywriters are the engine of the creative team because they're "word people" and can explain the work better and more rationally that those magic marker–wielding Art Directors. One Art Director I know always complained that clients never looked him in the eye when discussing the work. Throughout his career, from his humble roots in the bullpen at Doyle Dane Bernbach in the sixties to many stints at topnotch agencies in New York City, he found that clients almost always directed their questions and comments to his copywriting partners. Little did they know that nearly every headline in his award-winning portfolio and most of the taglines were written by him. So clearly, he knew a little bit about language! Once, when his partner was unable to go to a major client pitch, he delivered the presentation solo—and returned back to the agency with a $50-million account. The president of the agency was so happy that he kissed him smack on the lips.

In fact, here's a list of famous Art Directors who went on to establish their own agencies—another clear indication that those magic marker–wielding Art Directors really do know something about the business needs of clients:

George Lois (Lois Calloway)

Rich Silverstein (Goodby, Silverstein & Partners)

Jay Chiat (Chiat Day)

Roy Grace (Grace and Rothschild)

Alex Bogusky (Crispin Porter + Bogusky)

Sam Scali (Scali, McCabe, Sloves)

Ralph Ammirati (Ammirati Puris)

David Kennedy (Wieden + Kennedy)

While we're at it, here are a few Copywriters who also have their name on the door:

Bill Bernbach (Doyle, Dane, Bernbach)

Ed McCabe (Scali, McCabe, Sloves)

Linda Kaplan Thaler (Kaplan Thaler Group)

Diane Rothschild (Grace & Rothschild)

Martin Puris (Ammirati & Puris)

Carl Ally (Ally Gargano)

David Ogilvy (Ogilvy & Mather)

Dan Wieden (Wieden + Kennedy)

Jeff Goodby (Goodby, Silverstein & Partners)

BTW: *Adweek* named Copywriter Jeff Goodby and Art Director Rich Silverstein "Executives of the Decade" in 2010. How's that for a couple of Creatives?

Story Number Four. Here's another "stereotype within a stereotype" story. I was the Copywriter of a Folgers coffee commercial that ran every Christmas for 20 years. It was the story of a college-aged son who unexpectedly comes home for the holidays and awakens his family by brewing a pot of coffee. The scenario was inspired by my wish to see my older brother, Peter, who hadn't come home for Christmas in five years. Many of the details in that spot came from my childhood memories: the houseful of relatives, the holiday decorations, even the fact that our Christmas tree lights were connected to the light switch in the hall. One thing that this spot didn't include: dialogue. With the exception of a small exchange in the first 15 seconds (written by my supervisor—who was an Art Director), this commercial contained no words. So many people, including other Creatives in the agency, often referred to this spot exclusively as my Art Director's. We'd often be standing together and people would say, "Nice spot, Josh." After all, he was the Art Director. And aren't they the "picture people"? I never personally regarded the commercial as either his or mine. It was always "ours." But I did find it interesting that, for many people, the lack of copy in the commercial made me a secondary player. So the Art Director/Copywriter stereotypes cut both ways. (BTW: after the commercial aired the first year, my brother, Peter, did surprise me by coming home for Christmas.)

Story Number Five. To recalibrate your perceptions even further, here's the story of a real creative type who wouldn't need a denim shirt to prove he's in the creative department. This guy dropped out of college, but stuck around campus so he could audit classes such as calligraphy where he learned the art of kerning letters. He traveled to India as a young man in search of spiritual enlightenment, returning as a Buddhist with a shaved head. Now in his mid-fifties, he is rarely (if ever) seen in a tie and even attends important business meetings in a beat-up pair of jeans. He would have definitely fallen under the category of Art Director or Copywriter in the exercise you did earlier. But the guy I'm describing is Steve Jobs, the chairman and CEO of Apple. He's the one who hired the ad agency, Chiat Day, that created the famous "1984" commercial introducing Macintosh personal computers to the world. So he's a client with a capital "C." Yet creative? Totally. And most likely equipped with killer critique skills. That's one reason why Apple advertising is among the most memorable on the planet: Both agency and client know how to talk about the work . . . and to each other.

Two Sides to Every Stereotype

So let's go down a basic list of descriptors that defines the creative/business divide and see if there's not at least two different ways of looking at the same personality trait.

Who are these CREATIVE Professionals...?

They're slobs. | They're nonconformists.

They're oddballs. | They're expressive.

They're exhibitionists. | They know how to attract attention.

They're artistic. | They're smart. (Why do these tend to be opposing traits?)

They react with their gut. | They have street smarts.

They're brash. | They're colorful.

They're so pushy. | They're persuasive.

They're egotistical. | They're confident.

The way we behave and express ourselves is always open to interpretation. One person's pushy is another person's persuasive. But before you sit in judgment of Art Directors, Copywriters, or Creative Directors, consider what you expect them to deliver at the end of the day. Wouldn't most of the above adjectives make for pretty decent ads? You want your ads to be confident and persuasive. You want your ads to call attention to themselves. You don't want them to look like everyone else's. Of course, you don't want to get obnoxious about it—being persuasive is definitely better than being pushy. But still, all ads need some creative heft in order to get noticed and be successful. It seems logical, then, that these traits would also exist within the people who actually create the ads. Even the more annoying expressions of these traits may be worth harnessing in order to achieve everyone's mutual goal of producing great work. And if, perhaps, you could try to recalibrate some of your initial, knee-jerk appraisals, perhaps that will be your reward.

Now let's take a look at the business side of the aisle. There are two sides to this coin, too.

Who are these BUSINESS-MINDED Professionals...?

They're rigid.| They're buttoned up.

They're anal. | They're analytical.

They're predictable. | They're methodical.

They lack "street smarts." | They're "book wise."

They're scared. | They're pragmatic.

They're artistically challenged. | They're research oriented.

They're straight-laced. | They're professional.

They're reactive. | They address what's in front of them.

Of course, there's the same negative and positive spin on each of these, too. But notice that there's also a yin and yang quality when you put this whole list next to the creative list. It seems that no matter who's interpreting what, there's a nice balance here. A true complimenting of talents. On the bright side of things, you could easily describe the creative/management relationship in the same way that Le Corbusier described New York: "It is a catastrophe . . . a beautiful catastrophe."

So in order to optimize this important relation and to make the most of creative and management collaboration, should we put on the kid gloves or take out the boxing gloves? The answer is: neither. We should all respect each others' particular talents. We should expect those on the management side to look beyond the numbers and not try to quantify everything. We should come to expect Creatives to have the discipline to be problem solvers and designers, not freewheeling artists and auteurs. Appreciate their special temperaments, but not indulge their temper tantrums. Remember, we're not just professionals but grown-ups, too. This is common ground upon which we can all firmly stand.

 Visit the student study site at www.sagepub.com/tagstudy for additional online resources including web links, video clips, and recommended readings to learn more about advertising and the creative process.

Critique Exercises

1. Present an advertising campaign in three different ways: as an Art Director, as a Copywriter, and as an Account Manager. Examine how you articulate and defend the work differently depending on your relationship to the ad.

2. Write a 200-word essay on any of the listed people on pages **145–146** and focus on their approach to selling great work to their clients.

Suggested Reading

While there are various players in the ad game, it's the work—or the big idea—that's really king. No matter who's at the table, this is something that everyone can rally around. Here are some books that help you value the idea as the great unifying force.

• *The Art of the Idea,* by John Hunt, talks not only about the power of ideas but also about our relationship to ideas . . . which is at the heart of critique. Reveals how all people, whether they're creative professionals or business-minded professionals, can be empowered by opening up to more conceptual thinking. http://www.theartoftheidea.com/

- *The Idea Book,* by Fredrik Härén, is a business book about creativity and seeks to unite both sides of the divide through creativity. http://www.theideabook.org

- *The Creative Process Illustrated,* by Deborah Morrison and W. Glenn Griffin, does a great job of getting you inside the heads of Creatives—and shows you the process through illustrations done by actual Art Directors and Writers.

AdSpeak Up!

Who Says What When

"Timing is everything."

When it comes to critique, it's not just about knowing what to say but when to say it. Good timing can save a lot of time and frustration. As with all things in life, sometimes the realization that something is wrong—or right—only becomes apparent after the fact and at the least appropriate moment. Most people feel more comfortable being REactive to finished work than PROactive while work is in process. That's why it's important to train ourselves to match our voice to our opportunities. A basic appreciation of the process and how your contribution matters will not only make your critique more valuable but also make you more valuable to the process. This is the best way to become the indispensible, go-to person who everyone wants at the meeting.

The Cast of Characters

The Brand Team, AKA "The Client": played by a bunch of folks in the marketing department of a company.

The Account Team: played by the bunch of people who manage the account on the agency side and, along with the Strategic Planners, give direction for the creative product.

The Creative Director: played by someone who has risen from the ranks of either Copywriter or Art Director and supervises the creative process.

The Creative Team: played by the Art Director and Copywriter, this is the two people who have actually created the advertising.

The Basic Chronology of the Process

STRATEGY   >   CONCEPT   >   EXECUTION   >   LAYOUT   >   PRODUCTION

You may recognize these as basic terms from AdSpeak, so we don't need to define them here. However, let's see how they might be expressed on this timeline, what the value of critique is at each stage, and who says what when.

Strategy

The strategic document usually takes the longest to develop. It relies on market research and often goes through more than one phase of testing. Depending on what type of project it is, strategic platforms might be created. Sometimes called "adlobs," or ad-like objects, these are consumer-friendly forms of trying out a strategy. It's easy to confuse these with concepts; indeed, some treat them as one and the same. But in most cases, they should be considered part of strategic development, not creative development—even when the creative team is involved. At the end of this phase, all the research and testing results are distilled into a tidy document like so:

MCA.363 /ADVERTISING COPYWRITING
Sample Creative Strategy Statement

Client/Product: Bazooka Bubble Gum
Date: 6 October 2009

Student: Nancy Tag

PRODUCT DESCRIPTION
    In REALITY: a bubblegum introduced in 1947, interactive, sweet, fun, blows good bubbles, has problems appealing to adults, newer bubble gums are tough competition, 5 cents a piece
    As PERCEIVED: All American, childish, too sweet, hard to chew, fun
    The COMPETITION: Double Bubble, Bubblicious, Bubble Yum

Why are we advertising?
The problem is: bubble gum is a kid's candy which means that Bazooka is continually losing its core consumer (after all, kids grow up) and Bazooka must keep re-building brand awareness for its ever-changing target.

What's the main message of the ad campaign?
The COMMUNICATION OBJECTIVE is: to convince older people that Bazooka Bubblegum Gum is a great stress reliever for adults.

Who are we talking to?
The TARGET AUDIENCE is: *Demographically*, we're trying to reach professional men and women over the age of 25, college educated, income of $30,000+.

Psychographically, we're interested in appealing to people who are overwhelmed by the responsibilities of adulthood and who would like to remain young-at-heart.

>> *Reasons to Believe*
    The BENEFIT to the consumer is: blowing Bazooka Bubble Gum is so silly and childish that it's a fun way to relax.

    The product can SUPPORT this because: as you'll recall from your youth, Bazooka blows a mean bubble. The sugar is an immediate rush. Plus, the act of blowing helps breathing which is a physical stress reliever. Also, it's scientifically proven that the color pink makes people happy – which helps lower anxiety.

    Note: this is a format, not a guideline. Please follow it exactly.

The strategic document is a great catalyst for critique. Since so many strategic discussions occur during its development, once it's distilled into a single document, it's much easier to determine whether the right insights have been selected, if all the elements hang together, and if it's a viable and distinctive direction for creative development.

Who Says What When

> **The Client,** of course, initiates the strategy and provides preliminary input and research to the agency.
>
> **The Account Team,** which includes Strategic Planners, takes initial input from the client, but is the true engine behind the strategy. Members of account management touch base with the client to ensure that the strategy is on the right path. They also touch base with Creative management to ensure that the strategy can be turned into advertising. Once it's a tight document, the major managers in the process get an opportunity to critique the strategy before it's finalized. After revisions, it must be signed off by those same managers before the Creative Team begins their work.
>
> **The Creative Director** gives input to the Account Team to ensure that the strategy can be turned into effective advertising.
>
> **The Creative Team** generally receives the strategy in its finished form without being given the opportunity to critique it. However, sometimes the work reveals weaknesses in the strategy and leads to adjustments.

Concept

Next comes conceptual development. In this phase, the creative team starts thinking how to turn the strategic document into something that the consumer can relate to and interact with. This is when lightning strikes and big ideas percolate. Sometimes, the clients don't see the concepts; they just see rough comps of executed campaigns. Within the agency and especially within the creative department, concepts are shown as rough tissues that look something like this:

Rough tissues are simple line drawings done on tracing paper. They shouldn't feel finished because the thinking isn't solidified. There shouldn't be a lot of detail on the page because the particulars of the execution haven't been figured out yet. I've always wished that agencies had more faith in their clients' ability to understand rough tissues. But whenever a meeting approaches, there's this irresistible temptation to pretty everything up. And sometimes, it's the prettiness that gets in the way of fully appreciating an idea. As a creative director, I'd never let Art Directors go near a computer while they were working out ideas. I found that they'd get too seduced by some Photoshop tool or design doo-dad and forget that it was the idea that really mattered. Design comes later. Thinking comes first. And a rough tissue is good enough for that. Too bad we don't let the clients see more of it.

The concept phase is when there should be a discussion on how well the idea delivers the strategic message. There should be some critique on how compelling it is and how well the target will relate to it. There should be some discussion of how much impact such a concept will have in its media environment and whether it will make an engaging, sustainable campaign. At this point, there can be thoughts on how elastic the concept is: Can

it translate into different media outlets? The concept can also be examined to see if it fits into the brand personality.

Who Says What When

<u>**The Client**</u> doesn't do much during this phase.

<u>**The Account Team**</u>—depending on its relationship with the Creative Team—either stays as far away from the process as possible or stops by on occasion so the Creatives can bounce ideas around to determine if they're hitting the strategic mark.

<u>**The Creative Director**</u> also keeps his or her distance during the conceptualizing phase but sees the ideas once the Creative Team has them in rough tissue form to determine their viability, give critique, and kill what doesn't move forward.

<u>**The Creative Team**</u> is who does the conceptualizing. Some teams are high energy and spit out ideas in rapid fire. Others sit staring out the window for days waiting for inspiration. If someone from the Account Team walks in and has an expectation of which approach is more productive, he or she could be disappointed. The Creative Team immerses themselves in this process in their own way—give them a wide berth.

Execution

Next comes executional development. Sometimes, concepts and executions are conceived simultaneously. Sometimes, executions or an executional element is the first thing to come to mind, and the Creatives end up backing into the concept. The process is not entirely linear because thinking isn't. Especially in the creative realm. However, in a typical timeline, the execution of a campaign follows the concept. Here's how the execution for the earlier concept might look:

As you can see, the "invented stain" has been executed as a stand-alone object—as opposed to an object in situation—against seamless and graphically bold. In order to emphasize the inventive quality of this stain-producing object, the main headline gives the object a weird name: "The BBQ Grassberry Stain." The subhead summarizes how Wisk will deal with it—simply: "Yeah, we'll get that out."

(If this were a television spot instead of a print ad, the execution would come in the form of a storyboard.)

Who Says What When

The Client sees the work for the first time at this stage in the form of tight comps. That's because that agency can't spend money on photographers, typographers, retouching, and so on that is required to create original ads until the client signs off on the comps and approves a budget. Because we live in the age of Photoshop and it's easy to manipulate stock photography, sometimes a comp can look like a fully produced ad. This is great for getting the client onboard for swift approvals. However, this approach can compromise the final product. It's too easy to become wedded to good-looking comps (short for "composites") and not push for a higher level of originality further on in the process. A better approach is to present more rough, illustrated comps, such as the one above.

Because this is the first time that the Client has seen the work, it's important for the Creative Team to present their work explicitly and engagingly. It's also important to allow the Client to critique the work without feeling intimidated. Before exposing the advertising to the Client, the agency has been living with it for a while. So not everyone at the table is on the same level of familiarity.

The Account Team is often asked to wait until the execution phase before seeing the work. That's simply because it's easier to understand and critique at this phase. Allowing folks outside of the Creative Department to see rough concepts is risky because it requires a level of "ad literacy" that's often limited to other Creatives. However, the Account Team's input is critical. So as soon as the executions have been approved within the Creative Department, they're presented to all levels of management to determine if they've met strategic objectives. If not, the Creative Team needs to rework the comps. Without the nod from account management, the ads will not be presented to the client.

The Creative Director looks at executions to see if they've delivered on their conceptual promise and still meet strategic objectives. This is when the finer points of the execution are finessed before the work is allowed to leave the department. Sometimes the Creative Director will accompany the Creative Team when the work is presented to the Account Team. He or she will often be at the Client presentation either to make the actual presentation or to support the work.

The Creative Team presents the executed advertising to the Creative Director, the Account Team, and the Client. At each presentation, they must be able to engage in critique and defend their work and/or make adjustments. If the Creative Team is not good at presenting and critique, their immediate supervisor ends up presenting their work to the major players in the process. Therefore, the more skillful Art Directors and Copywriters are at presentation and critique, the more control they'll have over their work.

During the executional phase, critique focuses on how well the execution delivers on the concept and if both the concept and execution are strategic. Is the communication clear? Are the headline, tagline, and body copy working as hard as they can? Is this the best presentation of the imagery? Do the visual and the text work together as strongly as they can? Sometimes you don't know if a concept is viable until you see it executed. Sometimes, the execution forces the concept to evolve. Therefore, conceptual arguments can still be made at this point. Even errors in strategy can become apparent during this phase. Sometimes, creative teams complain that clients are changing their minds or are being reactive rather than proactive when the strategy shifts during execution. In theory, that's true. However, sometimes even the best strategy can be proven wrong once the actual work comes to life.

Critique during the execution phase should also include preproduction comments, such as how will the photo(s) be shot and/or what will the design elements look like once they're produced? How will they support the communication and enhance the page?

Layout

Next, the Art Director finesses the finer points of the execution into a layout. Usually, the layout has been carefully considered before the ads are first presented to the client. But until all the elements are generated, such as the original photography and/or design elements, it's impossible to fully know what the layout will look like.

(THE BBQ GRASSBERRY STAIN)

Yeah, we'll get that out.

Introducing Wisk Away

(If this were a television commercial instead of a print ad, the layout phase would be comparable to a shooting board in which the director explains camera angles, lenses, and character development.)

Who Says What When

Critique at the layout stage usually revolves around how elements relate to each other. Is the headline too far away from the subhead? Is the main visual too small? Should we bump up the tagline? If you're far along in the layout phase, making strategic, conceptual, and executional comments isn't that productive at this point. Make those earlier. Not here.

> **The Client** sees the layout before approving the ad for its final phases of production.
> **The Account Team** needs to approve the layout before it is shown to the Client.
> **The Creative Director** needs to approve the layout before it is shown to the Account Team.
> **The Creative Team** finesses the layout. The Copywriter needs to proofread the copy and make sure the lines are broken for best communication. The Art Director determines where all the elements on the page work best and reviews camera angles with the photographer before the shoot. The creative team critiques each aspect of the layout as they work toward the most effective communication.

Production

There may be some critique during the actual production of an ad, but only about certain aspects of production. For example, there can be some debate over how the product is being filmed or how an illustrated element is being drawn. These things can be connected back to strategic objectives. Or how well they bring the concept to life. However, this isn't the point to discuss the merits of the strategy or the concept. The time for that is over. When preparing the ad for publication, critique turns more into an issue of quality control. This is not the time to challenge the body copy, for example. But you can still proof and fix typos.

Who Says What When

> **The Client** is often present when the photographer is shooting a main visual in an ad. Or when the director is shooting the scenes in a commercial. They are there for a reason: to assess what's going on and make sure it captures what has been promised. This is a form of critique. However, it's also important for the client to appreciate that professionals are at work; their artistic vision needs to be respected.
> **The Account Team** also needs to assess and critique what's going on during the production phase, but it's also important for them to manage the Client here. It's a delicate process. There's a lot of money on the line, so it's important to speak up. On the other

hand, this is really the time to allow the artistry of the professionals to come to life. Since the Account Team is more comfortable with the process than the Client is, they need to raise their comfort level. Listen to their concerns, but also offer perspective.

The Creative Director oversees aspects of the process but generally lets the Creative Team do its job. However, the Creative Director does need to give a critique of the final product before it can be published or aired.

The Creative Team oversees every aspect of production. The Art Director and Copywriter are responsible for critiquing the work of all the professionals in the process: photographers, typographers, film directors, editors, music composers, colorists, and so on. Now the tables have turned; in the same way that the Client and Account Team had to assess and critique how well the Creatives' campaign delivered on strategy, now the Creative Team must assess and critique how well all their production partners are delivering on the Creative Team's campaign concept, execution, and strategy. Suddenly, the Creative Team has become the ambassadors of the brand. They need to diplomatically harness the enormous talents of their production partners for the purposes of their campaign. Fortunately, they have well-oiled critique skills to help them out.

While this timeline is more specific to developing print advertising, the basic chronology applies to most forms of advertising. Of course, some of the particulars will be different depending on both the breadth, degree of integration, and the media platforms of your campaign.

 Visit the student study site at www.sagepub.com/tagstudy for additional online resources including web links, video clips, and recommended readings to learn more about advertising and the creative process.

Critique Exercise—in Four Parts

In order to experience how critique changes depending on what phase of the process you're in, generate original ads over the course of a few weeks.

1. Week One: Select a product and write a basic strategy that includes the communication objective (the WHAT) and the target audience (the WHO). Using this strategy, create at least three rough tissues, each one representing a campaign concept (the HOW). Present each concept by taping the rough tissue to the wall, stating the WHAT, the WHO, and the HOW. Describe possible executional approaches. Then open the floor to critique.

2. Week Two: Based on the critique deconstructing how well your concepts delivered the strategic message and spoke to your target, select the best campaign concept and expand it into a campaign of three ads. Re-present your work, being more specific about the executional elements in each ad. Open the floor to critique.

3. Week Three: Based on the critique that deconstructed how well your execution paid off your concept and delivered your message, finesse the executional elements and layout. Re-present your work. Open the floor to critique.

4. Week Four: If you're a capable designer, take the layout to the highest level of production. Re-present. Open the floor to critique.

Throughout this process, take note of and discuss when certain comments can be best addressed substantively or superficially. For example, a critique that questions the strategic message in Week Three may seem inappropriately timed—the presenter would feel justified in responding that this comment should've been made earlier. However, certain aspects of how the strategy is being expressed can be made at all stages of creative development. For example, does the typeface in the layout truly fit the message? Will the target be pulled in by the lead-in line of the body copy? And so on. Evaluate the productiveness of each critique based on the stage of creative development in which it's presented.

CHAPTER 8

The Creative Team's Bill of Rights

I believe in an open mind, but not so open that your brains fall out.

—Arthur Hays Sulzberger

Now that we've discussed ways to bridge the creative/management divide and see each other in a more compatible light, it's also important to figure out productive ways to keep our distance and retain the core essence of what we do. Yes, we're all creative. And yes, we all possess business acumen. Still, there are distinctions that need to be appreciated and acted upon accordingly. Creativity and commerce do not flourish in the same type of environment. They are not always motivated by the same things. In the hallways of an ad agency alone, the distinctions are manifest: The account management floor is often more staid and polished; the creative floors whiff of chaos and color. How do we operate as individuals and yet still function in this partnership? Just like the Founding Fathers did. With a bill of rights. That way, no matter which side of the divide you associate yourself with, we can both treat each other with respect. This guarantees ample freedom, without trampling on each others' inalienable rights. It liberates and provides discipline, all at the same time. It's a great way to do business, especially when the business involves dynamic parts of art and commerce.

As with most of *Ad Critique,* let's focus here on the Moment of Truth: the creative presentation. This is when the creative/management divide is most apparent; indeed, they physically sit on opposite sides of the room, often with a very large table between them. This is when the personality types become most exaggerated and are therefore less likely to harmonize. There's also much at stake so tensions are running high. That's why we should all familiarize ourselves with . . .

The Creative Team's Bill of Rights: Eight Things Every Art Director and Copywriter Have a Right to Expect During the Presentation of Their Work

This is "mandatory reading" for any business-minded person who's evaluating creative work. That means Brand Managers, Account Managers, and so on. Consider this list a guideline. A template of behavior. The rules of engagement. But as the name suggests, this bill of rights is really for the benefit of the creative team. I know. You guys don't like rules. But trust me: If all the "suits" read this before your presentation, they'd have a level of comfort that would finally allow them to be uncomfortable—which is that place where great creative work happens. This allows the work to move forward rather than stopping dead in its tracks. And that's something we can all agree on.

Amendment One

It is within The Creative Team's rights to present their work to clients who are alert, open-minded, and responsive.

Seems like a no-brainer. But it's not. You'd think that if a client asked for work, he or she would be eager to receive it. Yet in my career, I've come across way too many clients and account folk who don't want to like the work, even before you've entered the room. I've had clients fall asleep during presentations . . . and snore (of course, in some Asian countries, this could actually be a sign of dominance).

There are an infinite number of reasons why. Some of them have to do with sleep deprivation. Others are based on pure defensiveness (when in doubt, don't pay attention. Or sit stone-faced and unreceptive so no one knows you're confused). Once in a while, clients are frustrated Copywriters and have already envisioned the work before even agreeing to a strategy. Therefore, the work is always wrong . . . because it's not what was inside their heads. And then there are those people who are just born to be negative.

The bottom line here is that when management sits down at the table, they should keep a firm eye on the strategy but be open-minded in terms of how it's expressed. Don't walk in with preconceived notions. If you've already imagined what the outcome should be, suppress it. Allow yourself to be surprised.

Amendment Two

It is within The Creative Team's rights to be able to make a full presentation of their work before it is prematurely judged.

As I instruct all my students, a presentation should tell a story. They should all have a beginning, a middle, and an end. The work can't exist in a vacuum. It must be set up, described, displayed, then sold. When the folks sitting on the other side of the table jump to conclusions, interrupt, or stop the Art Director or Copywriter before the presentation is over, they are depriving themselves of the work's context and the creators' insight. In that case, the judgment is being based on insufficient data. Lots of clients say, "I'm just reacting to the way the consumer will see the work: immediately." That's ridiculous. Of course, we all have to keep the end user in mind whenever we judge advertising, but as the professionals who actually produce the work, we need to bring more skill sets to the table. And the first one—the one that is the prerequisite to critique—is the ability to listen . . . thoroughly. Patiently. Receptively.

I once saw a client walk out on a presentation when the Creative Director was 10 words into it. This is not a good way to foster a productive relationship or get good advertising. On the other hand, I once had an Account Executive give my work a standing ovation before I even finished reading the headline. As flattering as this was, it didn't do the work any good in the long run. We're all responsible for selling the work up and down the line at some point in the process. If we don't spend a good deal of time really trying to understand it, we can never truly be its advocate. The best time to learn about the work is when the creative team is making the presentation.

Amendment Three

> It is within The Creative Team's rights to exchange views in a hostile-free environment that encourages spirited debate, proper consideration, and constructive analysis.

Once I plowed through an impressive dog-and-pony show for a new client who couldn't keep the smirk off his face. When I was done, he asked me to flat-out leave the building. By way of explanation, he told me that it wasn't me. Or the work. He just hated his boss who had promised his account to my agency behind his back (and on the golf course). Of course, his boss wouldn't allow him to terminate the relationship. This pretty much guaranteed that every presentation would go the same way. Not only was every presentation torture, but it affected the work going in and coming out. We continued to churn out advertising, but we did it without enthusiasm and with resentment. When the client bashed what we did, we didn't fight back. Who cared? When he liked the work, we saw no reason to build on his comments to improve it further. Who cared?

Another client I knew used the creative presentation as an excuse to bully his own subordinates. He always took a neutral posture throughout the presentation, masking any indication of whether he liked or loathed the work. When the presentation was over, he'd ask the management chain, one by one and in order of seniority, what they thought. They'd all stammer at first, trying to anticipate the "right" response. Ultimately, though, they'd go into default mode with some vague variation of "I don't like it." The fewer details they offered, the better; any evidence that they were capable of thinking for themselves was just another opportunity for their boss to demean them. Of course, "I don't like it" is not much of a critique and quite unhelpful to the creative team. But we had to endure hearing it, again and again. Finally, the senior client would take the floor and that's when we'd get a real earful. Not about the work, mind you. That was clearly secondary here. It was more of a rant about what a bunch of lug heads he had working for him. Oh, yeah. And he didn't like the work, either. This was always quite a performance, better than anything the agency could've put on. And it was so predictable that we knew it had little to do with our work but with our client's relationship to his own employees. Needless to say, nothing was ever accomplished at these meetings. The advertising always ended up being pretty mediocre—although better than they deserved. We all dreaded seeing that client and often drew straws to determine which one of us would have to suffer through the next meeting. Trust me, a clear sign that the client/agency relationship is in bad shape is when your meetings are only attended by Creatives who drew the short straws.

Here's a basic truth: Creative work is fragile. So it is critically important that it be presented in a fairly welcoming environment. It will not only make the presentation better, but will improve the quality of the work. When the Art Director and Copywriter know that their supervisors, Account Managers, and clients are eager to see the fruits of their labor, The Creative Team is more likely to work harder, longer, smarter—not just to please the client but to wow them. To impress them. To take risks.

Don't misinterpret this to mean that Creatives need to exist in some sort of "happy bubble." Most Art Directors and Writers don't mind having the client challenge their work if the questions are informed and indicate that everyone's fully engaged in the process. Don't avoid spirited debates because you're afraid of hurt feelings. It makes the work better, and no self-respecting creative will back away from a chance to defend his or her ads. In addition, if there is a palpable sense that each party is motivated by a sense of excellence, even a heated argument feels productive. Creatives don't need you to love everything in order to feel successful. Certainly, it's great when work is loved (and please be effusive in your praise if it's merited). But being appreciated for your work and your process is an even richer, more sustaining reward. If work gets rejected—and everyone's work gets rejected—a more positive presentation environment makes it easier to go back to the drawing board.

It all comes down to creating a balanced relationship built on respect and trust. While Brand Managers and Account Executives need to be mindful of the creative temperament (see Amendment Six), they don't need to walk on eggshells. Art Directors and Copywriters are actually a very resilient bunch. They're used to having their ideas shot down on a daily basis long before the client or account team gets involved—by their own personal standards, their partner, competing teams, their supervisors. They're used to defending their work. They're used to rejection. But only up to a point. So whenever possible, it's good to offset a generally anxiety-ridden process with a nurturing environment. Agency Creative Departments do it by putting pool tables and lounge chairs in their common spaces. Clients can do it by ensuring that the presentation space is embracing, not hostile, and that the management vibe is upbeat, not contemptuous. You don't need to create "I love it" zones. However, "let's make great work possible" zones are a good bet.

Amendment Four

It is within The Creative Team's rights to feel proprietary about their work and protective about the creative process.

Creatives love their work. From an emotional point of view, each comma and every corner of it is theirs. Ideas are born. Work is their baby. No matter who's paying for it or who has legal rights to it, the ads are theirs. Period. This is a good thing. Yes, it may seem irrational (this is a business, after all). It results in more possessive and defensive posturing during critique. It even makes some Creatives pugnacious. But no matter how uncomfortable this sort of attitude makes a client, he or she should also be happy about it. If the work is good, it truly IS defensible. As we've learned through the Language of Critique, the ability to pull things apart and justify them is not just laudable but critical to the creation of effective advertising. If Creatives can't defend their work, it's either because they're inarticulate in the ways of critique OR the work has no rhyme or reason. And since critique is the great leveler, business-minded professionals are more equipped to distinguish between hot air and substantive discussion.

Good work should be defended and fought for—not just from the people who've created it but by the people who want to produce it and profit by it. Indeed, discussion and critique make the work not only more airtight but more loveable—by everyone. Suddenly everybody starts to feels proprietary—not just the Creatives, but the client, the sales force, even your extended family. You'll see. It's a good feeling. And that's when you really appreciate that this is a good emotion to foster, not fear. So let the Creatives love their work. Let them want to win awards. There's nothing wrong with that passion. When you come across Creatives that don't feel this way, run in the other direction.

Hopefully, the Creatives' pride of ownership should spill over to everyone. One area, however, isn't up for grabs: the actual process of creation. After all, this is principally the domain of the creative team. This is where the action is; it's one big reason to hire one agency over another. So when a client or account executive starts tinkering around with the work—suggesting entirely new headlines for this ad, re-envisioning scenarios on that ad—Creatives may justifiably become testy and withdraw from the collaboration. The business-minded professional's best contribution to the process is not actually creating the product but being proficient at critique. Collaboration may be a hands-on activity—until the advertising starts to suffer from too much "group think." That's why setting boundaries is a smart idea. Good Creatives want a participatory and actively involved client, but that is quite different than a client who usurps the Creatives' role. That's simply counterproductive.

Here's an example of client who had "boundary issues." She effusively praised a radio script I had written, paid me for my work, then completely rewrote it without telling anyone—least of all me. It turns out that she was only using my work to get her own "creative juices" flowing. She then proceeded to cast the talent and book the recording studio. When the producer took it from there, he was stuck with a spot that made no sense, had no discernible organization, and was 90 seconds over length, an eternity in commercial-land. As the most egregious aspect of spot, the radio producer and the recording engineer spent hours hacking away at the word count. They did ultimately succeed at bringing the spot in on time, but only after going seriously over budget. The quality of the spot, however, was beyond repair.

Ever wonder why a Copywriter likes to keep some control over the process? Now you know.

Amendment Five

It is within The Creative Team's rights to expect that their clients can separate the big idea from the minutia and to address each issue in accordance with its significance.

Okay. The strategy took months to develop. The research went on for weeks. Now the Creatives are about to reveal the fruits of everyone's labor: the latest advertising campaign. Their presentation starts with the strategic setup and leads up to a killer creative rationale. The grand finale is the unveiling of a 360-degree campaign consisting of 10 national print ads, an interactive website, and a regional TV spot. They wrap up with a spectacular pitch on how the work meets strategic goals and will galvanize the target into action. The performance is over. The Creatives sit down with exhausted satisfaction and await the client's reaction with equal amounts of eagerness and dread. The first client speaks up: "I'm not crazy about the blue band at the bottom of the third ad. Shouldn't it be red?" Hmmm. The Creatives nod to acknowledge the concern but search the clients' eyes for something more. A second client speaks up: "Does the logo have to be that small? It looks a little small to me." Hmmm. The nodding stops. Heads begin to cock. The Creatives are now stunned into total silence, a weak smile frozen on their faces. The agency account executive breaks in, "Let's get into the specifics later. What do you think of the campaign?" Hmmm. Furrowed brows. A third client pipes up, "I hear Crocs are really hot. Can the little girl in the first ad be wearing a pair?" Finally, a fourth client steps in, "Would you mind leaving us alone so we can talk about the work without you being here?"

Clearly, this is not the type of response that the Creatives expected to hear. But it's more than inadequate; this scenario is insulting and unacceptable, and it does not meet the standard of professional behavior. Yet it happens time and again. The problem, of course, is the lack of critique skills. Without them, clients don't know what to say or when to say it. Comments tend to be nonproductive and/or ill-timed. At a "big picture" meeting, nitpicking minutia such as the size of the logo reveals real panic—obviously, the clients have no idea what they're looking at so they cling to the small stuff like a life preserver bobbing on the wide ocean. This is inexcusable. We're all professionals doing our job; knowing how to critique is everyone's responsibility and among the inalienable rights of the creative team.

The basic solution? Read this book. Put it into practice.

Amendment Six

It is within The Creative Team's rights to not feel invisible after the presentation is over.

Some clients really do feel squeamish about being around creative folks. They know they need their services but would prefer that they do their job and then slip the work under the door. I suspect that this has a lot to do with not knowing how to talk to them. They fear their "otherness." Moreover, it's difficult for most people to talk about work—especially in process—in front of the people most responsible for it.

I see this played out in the college classes that I teach. Early each semester, I ask students to rip out examples of ineffective ads from magazines and pin them to the wall. We then dissect them in order to figure out what went wrong. The students have a lot of fun with this exercise because bad ads can be so . . . well, entertaining. They are rarely at a loss for words. Even the shyest among my students can be merciless in their critique, finding lots of substantial issues that should have been resolved long before the ad was ever produced. A recurring question is "how could professionals allow this to happen?" My response is "because the people who participated in the process didn't have nearly as much to say as you all just did." My students find this a real copout. Aren't the people responsible for this ad professionals? They're in disbelief. Until, that is, they are called upon to critique the work of their fellow students. In process. And in person. Suddenly, these same kids who were merciless at pointing out every little weakness of fully produced ads become very taciturn and, not surprisingly, generous. The same comment is heard again and again: "I like it." Ask them to be more specific and most will say, "Everything. I like everything." Really? When pressed to make a more concerted effort to identify a weakness in the work, the room goes silent. If someone speaks up, no matter how gently their criticism is expressed, he or she finds it very difficult to look the presenter in the eye. Often, the comments are directed at me as though the presenter has suddenly become invisible—even though he or she may be only a few feet away.

Why is this? Because we feel as though anything negative is hurtful. And while sometimes it is, there's nothing more constructive and ultimately positive than tactfully pointing out what's wrong. Of course, tact doesn't come naturally to most people. To compound the problem, it's also something that we're rarely trained in.

So this is what we must learn to do: We need to become proficient in the Language of Critique because therein lie the tools of tact. But we also need to learn to give the feedback directly to the people to whom it matters the most: The Creative Team. This is all about starting a dialogue. Remember to think of the presentation not as a one-way form of communication but as the first part of a long conversation. When's the last time you started a meaningful conversation by staring at your shoes? Look the creatives in the eye. Use their first names. Nod your head when you listen. Smile.

Amendment Seven

> It is within The Creative Team's rights to be privy to all pertinent information prior to the presentation. In other words, happy surprises are welcome; ambushing is not.

There is no doubt that isolating Creatives from the day-to-day minutia of running an account is a good idea. They don't need to know about every single client conversation. They need their own bit of space to think, reflect, create. But that doesn't mean that they shouldn't be informed of details that will affect their work. This may seem self-evident, but I can't tell you how many times I've presented something in a meeting and then heard, "Didn't you tell her?" Tell me what? That the budget was reduced? That the product name changed? That entire job was cancelled? Yes. Yes. And yes. In that order.

This is when you realize that you aren't just being protected from the minutia—you're in "Exile for Being a Creative." You weren't important enough to tell. Or smart enough. Or everyone was afraid you'd yell at the bearer of bad news. Or you were being protected—let's just sprinkle some fairy dust and make believe it never happened. Whatever. Eventually, you'll find yourself in the meeting making a passionate presentation only to find out that it's wrong, wrong, wrong. Too expensive. Incorrect name. Unnecessary.

Creatives are professionals. Give them the information they need to get the job done. Don't waste their time. Don't humiliate them by not giving them all the tools they need to get the job right.

Amendment Eight

It is within The Creative Team's rights to be left alone and given time to think. Sometimes even minor changes require a bit of creative finesse. So don't expect a response to every issue and concern on the spot (or even overnight).

Living in the digital age has accelerated communication, but it hasn't necessarily increased the speed at which we think, become inspired, create. Contrary to their reputations as creative geniuses, Art Directors and Copywriters generally don't develop ideas overnight or come up with revisions on the spot. Just because the world has moved faster doesn't mean that the brain moves faster. Admittedly, it is certainly easier to throw a comp together, but the thinking process still takes time. One of my partners always joked that clients thought she had a "layout button" on her computer because they expected revisions as soon as she returned to her desk.

This last amendment may be one of the most important of all. The trampling of this right can't be ameliorated through critique (and you were beginning to think that critique could save the world!). But it is one of the most basic rights that any self-respecting Creative should come to expect. Great work takes time. So if you're the client, build "inspiration" into your schedule. If you're the project manager, include "contemplation" in the timeline. And keep the word *quick* away from the word *turnaround*. Getting something done yesterday might be impressive and even doable once in a while, but if you come to expect speed, also expect substandard work.

Recap

The Creative Team's Bill of Rights:

1. To present their work to clients who are alert, open-minded, and responsive

2. To not have their work judged until it is fully presented and explained

3. To exchange views in a hostile-free environment that encourages spirited debate, proper consideration, and constructive analysis

4. To feel proprietary about their work and protective about the creative process

5. To expect that their clients can separate the big idea from the minutia and to address each issue in accordance with its significance

6. To not feel invisible after the presentation is over

7. To be privy to all pertinent information prior to the presentation. In other words, happy surprises are welcome, ambushing is not.

8. To be left alone and given time to think. Sometimes even minor changes require a bit of creative finesse. So don't expect a response to every issue and concern on the spot (or even overnight).

 Visit the student study site at www.sagepub.com/tagstudy for additional online resources including web links, video clips, and recommended readings to learn more about advertising and the creative process.

Critique Exercises

1. Present work in process. During critique, encourage "negative" comments by making everyone point out at least three weaknesses of the work in front of them. Consider: What could be improved? What isn't clear? Is the strategy being convincingly delivered? Examine the phrasing to determine the most productive way to critique work that needs to be made stronger.

2. After a critique session, critique the critique. Have presenters point out which comments were most productive and determine new phrasing for comments that were unclear or not helpful.

The Client's Bill of Rights

Some Creatives have a tendency to see themselves as an isolating bundle of contradictions: hero, victim, maverick. Anyone who isn't an "idea generator" is the enemy; they are always the force for good. This might be great for their egos, but it's a fantasy that does little to foster goodwill and is often detrimental to the work. Here's a news flash for Creatives: Clients are complex people, too. So are junior account executives, project managers, everyone up and down the ladder who isn't you. Once in a while, it would behoove an arrogant Art Director or defensive Copywriter to get off his high horse and give the other side a boost into the saddle. This bill of rights should help the Creatives appreciate their role in making the client/creative relationship work. Account Managers have these unalienable rights, too. So to both sides of the table: Read away.

The Client's Bill of Rights: Six Things Every Client Has a Right to Expect During a Creative Presentation

Amendment One

> It is within The Client's rights to be fully briefed on how the creative work is an outgrowth of the strategy.

One of the great mysteries of our business occurs when the strategy is suddenly transformed into a piece of advertising. How all that research, those long hours of analysis, debate, and insight turn into such an artful form of communication can be mystifying to everyone. Except the Creatives. After all, they were there during the transformation. They're responsible for the work and have fallen hopelessly in love with it long before they enter the room and present it to management. To the client, though, it's something new and even magical, which gives the presentation an air of excitement and anticipation. Seeing an Art Director and Copywriter present the advertising is a little bit of show business. The Creatives know this and encourage a visceral reaction to their work. Why ruin the smoke and mirrors with too much talk? On with the show!

Well, a certain amount of mystery is good. But before the curtain rises and opinions are solidified, it's critical to back up to where it all began: the strategy. It's not just where the work began; it's the last time everyone in the room spoke the same language and came together in agreement. Starting a meeting on a note of agreement is always a good thing. While the agency account team is partly responsible for putting the work into a strategic context, it really falls to the creative team to connect the dots, explicitly and carefully.

As the yardstick by which the work is measured, discussing the strategy at this point in the process may take some of the Hollywood out of the presentation, but it adds objectivity to the assessment, making critique seem less personal and capricious. Including this at the front end of the presentation will pay off at the back end. There's no greater selling point than work that has met its strategic objectives. And it's not just salesmanship; it's the goal of effective advertising. No matter how amazing the work is, advertising needs to be strategic. So unless you consider the creative presentation a theoretical exercise, it's up to the agency to establish for the client how the work meets the objectives that everyone agreed to before the work began.

Amendment Two

It is within The Client's rights to have the executional parameters of the material unambiguously defined before it is presented.

In addition to giving the work a strategic context, it's also important for the Creatives to more concretely set up what the client will be evaluating. Because we live in the age of digital design, being explicit has never been more important since a hastily slapped together comp can look deceptively like a fully finished ad. Before clients fall in love with (or loathe) what they're seeing, the Creatives must state in the most painfully obvious terms what is it that they're about to show. Are they about to present a campaign? Or a series of single ads? Or a concept that needs further development but is being shown for directional purposes? Is this the third revision? Or the eighth? And what exactly are the changes that were made? You can't be too obvious. Or fundamental.

This may seem like unnecessary hand-holding, but it's not. The presentation can go seriously wrong if you assume too much from the beginning. For one thing, it's easy for clients to forget where they are in the process. While Creatives may have spent the time between meetings toiling away on the same project, the client probably has been spending his or her time doing lots of other things—such as tending to his or her business. On top of this, clients don't always know what they're looking at. The difference between raw and retouched art may be extremely apparent to the agency, but that's because advertising is its day-to-day business. It may seem like "stating the obvious" to point out the distinction between a rough cut and a finished spot or between a radio script and a storyboard, but it might actually be revelatory for the client.

Perhaps the most important reason for clearly setting up the work beforehand is because it's very difficult to "undo" first impressions. Without a proper setup, clients can easily jump to false conclusions about what they're seeing. And then you may never be able to talk them out of it. For example, we once showed a client a rough comp using a piece of bland stock photography. Our intention was to hire a great photographer to take an original photo, but we needed the client's approval first. We only casually mentioned this intention while showing the ad since we felt that the piece of stock photography was so obviously bland. Big mistake. We should have made the point much more emphatically; this would've properly framed how the client viewed it. But we didn't, and it was a big, unfixable mistake. Apparently, the client's wife looked a lot like most of the women you see in stock photography. He immediately fell in love with the comp. The ad's fate was sealed. If we had made a bigger issue of it from the get-go, we might have had a fighting chance of talking him out of using stock photography. But we were stuck. And so was he. The ad we produced was pretty bland. We eventually lost the business. I can't imagine that he stayed married much longer, either.

Amendment Three

It is within The Client's rights to have the concept behind the advertising clearly articulated and to be shown how the concept has been meaningfully executed.

When making a presentation, the Art Director and Copywriter should always break down the creative work using the most explicit terms possible. Regardless of a client's critique skills, the use of clear language aids in decoding the more mysterious aspects of the work and helps facilitate discussion. This is especially true when it comes to explaining the most elusive aspect of all: the campaign concept. The onus is on the Creatives to articulate not only a campaign's concept but how the concept gives birth to the execution, why the layout reinforces the execution, concept, as well as the strategic message, and so on. Considering the importance of the concept to the sustainability of any campaign, it's imperative that the Creatives not only be able to articulate it but make it understandable to others. After all, if the Creatives can't identify the concept, then who can?

In addition, Creatives need to practice a bit of humility and appreciate how difficult it is for others to grasp the concept of an ad concept (refresh your own understanding of it by rereading Chapter 2: AdSpeak). Work that backs up the explanation is a good thing. So is clear language and repetition, as long as you don't start sounding like a kindergarten teacher. Creatives too often blow through their ads assuming that everyone immediately "gets" it. While it's true that great ads need to communicate clearly, that doesn't always mean that the client or account executive will necessarily understand why. Explaining why is part of the Creative's job. Let's all appreciate that this can be tough stuff, especially on the first exposure. That's when clarity and patience are critical. The earlier the client and the agency on are the same page, the more productive the entire process will be.

One of my partners would sometimes panic during a presentation. Rather than setting up the work, she would find herself tongue-tied and simply place the ads in front of the client. Once, the client asked, "What am I looking at here?" She pointed to an area on the comp that featured a glass of orange juice and replied, "When we photograph this, there'll be a glint of sunlight on the rim." The room went silent. No one knew quite what to do with this piece of information. Our supervisor stepped in and backed up from this small detail by reviewing the strategy, the concept of the ad, and the executional approach. Before wrapping up, he mentioned the glint of sunlight—now explained within a context. He saved the meeting. And the ad, which did end up having a glint of sunshine on the glass of orange juice.

To see an example of a wonderful creative setup of work, watch the first season finale of the AMC series *Mad Men,* in which Don Draper, the Creative Director of the fictional ad agency, Sterling Cooper, pitches the Kodak account. He turns down the lights and shows images of his life using their new slide projector. By the time he finishes with the presentation, the concept behind their advertising concept is clear: The projector isn't a wheel of slides; it's a carousel taking our memories on a ride. After the presentation, the client leaves the room but then calls from the lobby to tell them that they've won the business. Their decision was made on the elevator ride down. That's what happens when you don't just show the work but you give it context, a reason for being, and get the client nodding along with you.

Amendment Four

It is within The Client's rights to be presented with a recommendation and a reason why.

Fact: When showing a range of work, clients rarely pick the agency favorite. Don't ask me why. It just is. So the general agency rule of thumb is, never present work you wouldn't want to produce. This lessens the odds of having a happy client and an unhappy agency. Despite the fact that clients rarely select the agency favorite, that shouldn't stop the agency from making recommendations—and it should be based on something meaningful, not fanciful. There are two basic reasons for this. First, an agency with a real point of view is an agency of real substance. Second, an agency that is willing to state that point of view reveals even greater strength and character. Don't think the recommendation is implicit in the presentation. The best work on the table is not always as obvious as you might think. State it clearly and articulate the underlying reasons why. If this isn't explicit, the client will have to read the agency's mind . . . and if the agency has opted *not* to give a recommendation, there's evidently not enough thinking going on in there for the client to read.

Creatives, especially, need to be prepared to have a firm and rational point of view on their work. Clients invariably ask, "Which one is your favorite?" immediately following the presentation. It's often a stall tactic. Or an attempt to gain popularity. Plus, they really do want to know. The worst thing that a Creative could say is "Oh, I like them all. They're like my babies." This gives the client the impression that he or she is not dealing with a professional. And that just reinforces the belief that Creatives are driven more by emotional whim than by sound strategic thinking.

Furthermore, the Creative Department and the Account Management Department must agree on the reco ahead of time and the reasons why. No matter how discordant things may be at home, it's important to have a united front for the client. This sounds quite obvious, but it's not always done. Being conflicted (or at least revealing your conflicts) in front of the client is confusing—and doesn't make the agency look good.

I once attended a pitch with my agency president when the clients asked—as they so often do—"Which campaign do you recommend?" The new business team had all been in total agreement back at the agency. However, none of us had shared this viewpoint with our president since he rarely participated in new business pitches. So when he showed up, I figured he was on board, too. Without hesitation, the two of us answered simultaneously—with different answers. This put me in a pickle. Do I defer to the agency president so he didn't look bad or push for the recommendation the rest of us had agreed to earlier? Of course, I quickly jumped in and said, "Well, we like them all. They're like our babies!" But then made a very rational case for why the agency recommendation was a better way to go. Once in a while, having it both ways works.

Amendment Five

It is within The Client's rights to be given an opportunity to openly critique the work without intimidation, undue pressure, or unreasonable time constraints.

The creative presentation is, perhaps, the most inequitable moment in the agency/client relationship.

The agency works on a campaign for weeks, sometimes months before making a major presentation for a client. They enter the presentation room all dressed up, clearly rehearsed. They know the work inside and out. It looks good. With fancy artwork. Streaming video. Directors' reels. When the presentation is all over, they take their seats and stare at the client, waiting for a response. Well? Whaddya think?

The pressure to respond quickly and thoughtfully is enormous. But who's had time to absorb what they've just experienced, much less formulate a meaningful opinion? No wonder those on the client side of the table are often left speechless. Or make inappropriate comments. This is the exact moment when knowing the language of critique comes in handy. Armed with the words that will make a conversation productive, clients can jump right in. They can start the process of evaluation by asking the right questions. Rather than make an immediate assessment, they can probe the work. Look under the hood and see what's really going on. It puts the spotlight back on the agency. This way, the evaluation process can move more slowly and be more collaborative. No longer in the hot seat, the agency and the client can engage in a dialogue that more thoroughly explains the work. This also gives the client more time to digest it.

However, Amendment Five goes beyond the critique itself. It's also important that the agency—and especially the Creatives—set the tone in which critique can exist. This includes being forthcoming when questions are asked. Not defensive. Being instructive and detail oriented. This includes not expecting the client to say all the right things. The agency must allow them to put left-field comments on the table without a lot of eye rolling or heavy sighs. The client needs to hear their thoughts out loud—and so should the agency;

this gives the agency a chance to diplomatically counter what might have been left unsaid. The agency should not rush the client into coming to a conclusion. Persuasion is fine. The agency's role is to keep the comments on track, direct the more subjective responses back into a strategic framework, and reemphasize ways in which the creative work is effective. But undue pressure is not.

Years ago, I was once an unwitting participant in an amazing act of coercion after presenting a storyboard to the Aruba Tourism Board. The client was really enthusiastic about it so the account executive pulled out a production estimate and suggested that if he didn't sign it on the spot, the Copywriter—that would be me—wouldn't be available for the shoot because she—me, again—was six months pregnant. The client looked down at my belly, gave a quick glance at the production estimate, and immediately signed it. Generally speaking, I don't suggest pulling these sorts of stunts no matter how pregnant the Copywriter is.

Amendment Six

It is within The Client's rights to expect that Creatives will temper their passion with professionalism.

Creatives often complain that they don't get actionable feedback from the client. Sometimes, that's true because the clients are inept at critique and they're terrified of the Creatives. Other times, clients are quite good at critique, but they're still terrified of the Creatives. What are they afraid of? That "artistic" temperament. Nobody wants to be on the receiving end of a lunatic rant or the hysterical sobs of rejection. Of course, most Art Directors and Copywriters don't respond to criticism that way. But it's easy to believe in stereotypes. Therefore, it is up to the Creatives to assure the client that they're professionals who won't crumble or lash out during a meaningful critique. This means acting polite. Being receptive to well-intentioned comments. Not sounding condescending when explaining the work. Most people think that account management is responsible for all the relationship building that goes on between the client and the agency. But Creatives need to step up and build their own sort of relationships with the client, too. This doesn't mean that Creatives need to suddenly become all sweetness and pie. But building a moat between the client and their work is not a good idea, either.

Early in my career, I was a TV Producer and worked on a hideous project for a hideous Creative Director. He felt that because he had a special talent and won a few awards, he could terrorize everyone around him and they would tolerate his behavior. And they did. One day, I was leading a big preproduction meeting that included him, the client, the film director, and the creative team responsible for the storyboard. At one point, the Creative Director was not getting the response that he wanted and started to throw a tantrum. A real ugly, meltdown of a tantrum. His face got really red and he had trouble breathing. He kept saying, "I want it. I want it. I want it" over and over again—just like a toddler. He emphasized each word by banging both fists on the conference room table. The coffee cups jumped in their saucers to the beat of his fists. He finally stood up and stormed out. We were all stunned into silence. Few of us had ever seen behavior quite like that. Finally, the Copywriter cleared her throat and apologized to everyone on his behalf. "Oh, you don't have to apologize to *me,*" the film director said. "I just feel sorry for *you.* After this project, I don't ever have to see that idiot again. Unfortunately, you work for that guy and have to see him every day." His statement of the obvious changed my outlook. This was not creative behavior; it was simply bad behavior. And I never confused the two again. Bratty tyrants like that are jerks who don't deserve any respect. They're the ones who propagate the stereotype and give creative professionals a bad rap. Their work may be good. But it's never *that* good. No one's is.

There's no doubt that Creatives sometimes use their mystique to get attention. But when that mystique is abused and when Creatives become intimidating bullies, it's a barrier to healthy interaction and collaboration. They may win in the short term, but they won't build any relationships in the long run. It is within a client's rights to have the Creatives who work on his or her account behave like professionals. Period. End of story.

Recap

The Client's Bill of Rights:

1. To be explicitly shown how the creative work is an outgrowth of the strategy

2. To have the executional framework of the unambiguous material defined before it is presented

3. To have the concept behind the advertising clearly articulated and to be shown how the concept has been meaningfully executed

4. To be presented with a recommendation and a reason why

5. To be given an opportunity to openly critique the work without intimidation, undue pressure, or unreasonable time constraints

6. To expect that Creatives will temper their passion with professionalism

Suggested Viewing

AMC's series, *Mad Men,* Season One, Episode 13, "The Wheel." Or just watch the scene on YouTube http://www.youtube.com/watch?v = yWyLaXCV2_s. Consider why this presentation was so successful.

 Visit the student study site at www.sagepub.com/tagstudy for additional online resources including web links, video clips, and recommended readings to learn more about advertising and the creative process.

Critique Exercises

1. Post student work without presenting it. Ask half the class to critique it. Post the same work, but ask the creators to formally present it with a strategic setup and articulation of the concept and execution. Ask the other half of the class to critique it. Note the difference in the quality of the critique.

2. Have a student present three different campaigns to half the class without making a recommendation. Present the same three campaigns to the other half, but make a recommendation. Was the presenter able to influence the students based on the recommendation? Discuss how the outcomes were different and why.

CHAPTER 10

Presentation Prep

Critique happens all the time. In the back-and-forth banter of the Copywriter and Art Director. During the impromptu presentation of rough tissues when an account executive drops by the creative team's office. In late night brainstorming sessions. At presentations to your supervisor's supervisor. But the most high-stakes critique of all is the one that happens when the agency makes a formal client presentation to unveil a major campaign or important element of it. That's when strong critique skills can be used to help facilitate discussion and lead to productive solutions. Optimize this opportunity by making the environment as conducive as possible for fruitful critique, collaboration, and decision making.

Who's most responsible for making this happen? This is where account management really needs to step up and flex its muscle. If you're on the management side of the divide and ever feel relegated to the sidelines while the Creatives are busy doing their thing, channeling your energy into presentation prep is one of the smartest and most productive ways to contribute to the success of the project.

So for those really big creative presentations (and even some of those smaller get-togethers throughout the process), here are tips for some advanced planning that will help optimize the time that everyone spends together evaluating the work. Not everything is always in your control—but the more you *can* control, the better it is for you and the work.

Prior to the Meeting

1. Agree on a reasonable timetable for creative development (or appreciate the constraints and consequent compromises of an unreasonable one).

Few things irk a creative team more than having an unrealistic timetable imposed upon them. If it's really unreasonable, they'll waste more time grousing about the timetable than thinking about the assignment. While smart account executives and brand managers should have a basic understanding of how long any aspect of creative development takes, it's always wise to discuss that timetable with the creative team (or supervisor) before starting. Note the key words here of collaboration: *discuss* and *agree*.

Of course, establishing a reasonable timetable has a more direct impact on the actual development of the creative work, but it fosters a better, less adversarial relationship that then paves the way for a better meeting. It further serves as a reality check for the presentation. Appreciating the time constraints of creative development adds perspective. Knowing that the work was done under duress, for example, explains away some of the defensiveness oozing from the pores of the creative team. Appreciating the limitations of work produced on an unreasonable timeline can help frame the critique and make the Creatives feel less harshly judged.

2. Agree to provide significant information and insights at the *beginning* of the process instead of in drips and drabs *during* the process.

In other words, make the initial creative brief as complete as possible. When significant pieces of information are withheld or delayed, it does a real number on the creative team. It could turn a reasonable schedule into a rush job by invalidating weeks of thinking. Of course, no process is perfect. All decisions are based on insufficient data. Still, there are ways to optimize the process and not submarine the Creatives. Let's face it, there are lots of times when clients and account managers just want to "get the ball rolling" and purposely hand an assignment over to the creative team that isn't fully fleshed out. This is not an effective use of the Creatives' time. Plus, it undermines their trust in management. All briefs will be regarded with suspicion. When resentment runs high during the process, it will spill over to the presentation—and no amount of critique skills will make it go smoothly.

3. Agree that unexpected discoveries happen . . . and schedules need to be adjusted accordingly.

On the flip side, the advertising business thrives on the unexpected. If the process can't be open to new discoveries, we might miss out on something really special. So if important new information suddenly does reveal itself, everyone involved should be open to a possible game changer. If that's the case, also make sure that the schedule is modified so that everyone can make the most of the new revelation.

4. Agree on the explicit purpose of the meeting.

You know what happens when you assume. Yet many times, a bunch of people walk into a meeting with a bunch of different expectations about what the same meeting's supposed to be about. Invariably, someone will be disappointed—unnecessarily. I can't tell you how many times I've made a creative presentation only to hear something like, "That's nice, but I thought we were going to be looking at the media plan today." So make sure that every single person in the room knows exactly why he or she is there. Refresh everyone's understanding of where you all are in the process. Pinpoint how the meeting's function fits into that process. For example, is the meeting about reviewing concepts that are being revised . . . or completely new ideas? Was the campaign tweaked . . . or taken in a whole new direction—from an existing strategy? Revised strategy? New strategy? Is this a brainstorming session? Or a presentation of work? You can't be too explicit. It's as crucial as letting everyone know the date and time.

5. Agree on the form that the presentation material will take.

File this under: You can't state the obvious too obviously. That's life on a digital planet. We are now capable of creating "mood boards" with moving images and a fully mixed soundtrack to help establish a campaign concept. They're polished and beautiful in their own right. But if you don't reinforce ahead of time that the meeting is about conceptual thinking, the client may sit through the entire mood board wondering if you already went out and shot the commercial. Conversely, I like to present conceptual work that's as rough as possible so the client is entirely clear that we haven't yet entered the executional or production phrase of the process. However, if the client is used to seeing digitally produced comps that dance and sing, my rough sketches might look insultingly undone, no matter what the idea is behind them. So be clear about that upfront. These days, managing expectations must be balanced with the desire—and the digital capability—of wowing the client each step of the way.

The bottom line is this: Everything that you show to the client must have a reason why it's looking the way it looks. Moreover, the client needs to be aware of this prior to the presentation—not enough to take away the wow factor, but enough to ensure that the meeting won't end up as one big misunderstanding.

6. Agree on the limitations of the meeting.

We all have our limits. And so does the creative presentation. There are the limits of expectations. Limits of time. Limits of patience. It would be a good idea to talk about these things before sitting down to a meeting that already has its challenges. You can discuss the larger limits of strategy: "Let's remind ourselves that the campaign we'll be presenting will not sell cat food to dog lovers." You can discuss logistical limits: "We'll have a hard stop at 1:15 because we need to catch a plane back to Chicago at 3." You can focus on the limits of personality: "I know Ed sometimes gets antsy when the presentation goes beyond an hour. Should we prioritize the work so he sees the most important elements first?" Whatever the case, discuss these limitations ahead of time so that the meeting's limitations don't get in the way of productivity.

7. Make sure that everyone who will be attending the meeting is on the same page and has the same agenda.

At a very large creative presentation, there are many attendees who are not involved in the day-to-day business of the project. Therefore, not everyone will regard the work or project in the same way. What could've been a very productive meeting on a smaller scale now becomes a different animal. Many new or peripatetic attendees are simply out-of-sync with the process; the last time they dipped their toe in the water, they were further up the stream. When the head of the agency asks why he's looking at a rough cut that's been executed off a strategy that he thought he killed a few months ago, there's a possibility that he's been left out of the loop too long. No presentation could possibly go well after that. Therefore, getting everyone on the same page before such a major presentation is critical to achieving basic meeting equilibrium. Have your major disagreements in a different forum. Use the presentation to focus more directly on the work.

If you think getting everyone on the same page is difficult, try getting everyone to agree on the same agenda. That's a lot harder. These larger meetings have a strange mix of management levels with varying perspectives, senses of self-importance, and degrees of engagement. Some people may not fully appreciate their relevance to the project. They may have never supported the project from the get-go. Or they may have made some nasty prediction about the outcome that they'd prefer come true at all costs. Others may consider the meeting an opportunity to leverage some otherwise insignificant issue. This is a very political business, so it's not always possible to know what everyone's true agenda is. But that doesn't mean we can't make a reasonable effort to establish a common frame of understanding before the meeting begins. We may not reach full harmony, but a degree of transparency at least helps you position the work more advantageously.

8. Walk in knowledgeable.

Before you walk into the presentation room, know who's going to be in the room with you. Know their titles. Know their names. You can't sincerely look someone in the eye if you don't know who that person is. Make sure someone has given you a rundown of each person's importance in the presentation—and to you. There's no excuse for being ignorant of these basic facts; indeed, such ignorance can put the work in peril. I once knew a Copywriter who came into a meeting and accepted a cup of coffee from a woman; he assumed she must've been a secretary. So during the presentation, this Copywriter ignored her, figuring she had no say in the work. When he wrapped up, he was surprised that she was the first to speak. In fact, it turned out that she was the president of the company. Needless to say, she rejected the work—just as the Copywriter had rejected her. These types of stories play out from both sides. It's unnecessary drama and can be avoided if you just walk in knowledgeable.

Before you walk into the presentation room, know what you're about to present. Review the strategy. Review the work. Know it inside and out. Don't rely on notes. Or your partner. Or the assistant account executive. Don't think you can wing it. Know the work. Own the work. Be sincere. The better you know the work, the better you can defend it against any criticism or concern. The better you know the work, the more understandable it will be to others. It will seem worth the investment of time, energy, and resources. It's more worthy of respect.

Before you walk into the presentation room, know the background of the project. Why are you doing what you're doing? Who's got something to gain? Who's got something to lose? Is this a last-ditch attempt or another happy effort in a long winning streak? You don't need to overwhelm yourself with all the emotional baggage attached to any given project, but appreciating what's at stake for the people in the room will help you navigate the meeting.

Know your competition. Know the competition's advertising. Know the history of your product. Of your competition. Of the category. Be ready to use this information when you talk about the work; it's a necessary element in the art of persuasion—or dissuasion. You may not need to call upon this knowledge. But you never know. And knowing you know it will make you feel confident. Comfortable. And more able to engage in a productive dialogue.

Before you walk into the presentation room, know the presentation room. Where will everyone be sitting? What type of equipment will be there and can you rely on it? Figure out a way to position yourself in the room to the work's best advantage. If you're the person who's presenting, figure out where you'll feel most comfortable: at the front of the room? Next to the client? Standing? Sitting? A great creative director I knew spoke in a gentle, unhurried voice. He didn't feel right standing at a lectern presiding over a crowd. He was not a gesticulator or animated in any way. Whenever he presented his work, he always made sure to sit as close to the client as possible. He never projected his voice. He just spoke in measured, even tones. Everyone always leaned in to hear whatever he had to say. He was utterly charismatic—but only if he could take control of the room in a way that made him comfortable. Force him into another venue and this man of extreme self-assurance would crumble. For the sake of the work, the room was always set up so that he could take full advantage of his presentation style.

Recap

Presentation Prep:

1. Agree on a reasonable timetable (or appreciate the constraints of an unreasonable one).

2. Agree to provide significant information and insights at the *beginning* of the process instead of in drips and drabs *during* the process.

3. Agree that unexpected discoveries happen . . . and schedules need to be adjusted accordingly.

4. Agree on the explicit purpose of the meeting.

5. Agree on the form that the presentation material will take.

6. Agree on the limitations of the meeting.

7. Make sure that everyone who will be attending the meeting has the same agenda and is on the same page.

8. Walk in knowledgeable.

Visit the student study site at www.sagepub.com/tagstudy for additional online resources including web links, video clips, and recommended readings to learn more about advertising and the creative process.

Suggested Reading

Where the Suckers Moon, by Randal Rothenberg, which chronicles the pitch for the Subaru account and the subsequent campaign from Weiden + Kennedy, the chosen agency. It's filled with great stories of meetings, both big and small.

The Power of Nice, by Linda Kaplan Thaler and Robin Koval, is a sort of etiquette book on how to get along with all the people you'll meet in your professional life, from two high-powered bigwigs in the advertising business.

CHAPTER 11

Critique Cheats

Tips to Make the Most of the Critique

Okay . . . critique time is here. You feel proficient in AdSpeak. You know your AdErrors inside and out. And those AdAnalogies really nailed the synergy issue for you. But now judgment day is here and you're about to sit across the table from some smug creative type (or maybe even your own creative partner) who tends to get more defensive than a middle linebacker.

Relax. Remember that the point of a creative critique is not just about passing judgment but about opening up a meaningful dialogue. Is there a script to follow? It would be great if there were. But there isn't. However, the best way to start a critique is to ask questions. After all, we can't judge what we can't comprehend. Using AdSpeak to help you formulate these questions will not only make you look smarter but also result in more meaningful responses. As a fuller understanding of the work unfolds, the more deeply you can probe. Every aspect of effective advertising is "critique-able" because everything about an ad should have a raison d'être . . . a *strategic* raison d'être. So always circle back to strategic goals. It'll keep the conversation focused and help diffuse the inevitable subjective biases and emotionally wrought defensiveness.

One thing to bear in mind: Don't confuse critique with brainstorming. It can be a catalyst to brainstorming. But most presentations are not the time to come up with the creative solution but to measure what's in front of you against strategic goals. In other words, the presentation is more about the product than the process; that's best left to the creative professionals.

What's the best way to become good at critique? Practice, practice, practice. Look for opportunities to critique. Don't shy away from creative presentations. Start slowly. Even if you don't feel qualified to articulate your thoughts out loud, pull the work apart in your head. In fact, do silent critiques of the advertising that you see all around you: in magazines, on the TV, in bus shelters. Pay more attention to the ads on TV than to the shows. Formulate opinions. Try them out on your friends. Get comfortable with analysis. Don't settle for a brief summary. Go really deep. See how long you can sustain a discussion about a single piece of advertising.

Being good at critique isn't easy, but it's well worth it. People who are good at critique in their professional lives find great uses for it in their everyday lives. For example, an executive creative director I know from Deutsch just coached his son's little league to their first district championship in downtown Manhattan. What made him such a good coach? It's probably because he knew a little bit about baseball but even more about critique. My husband and I both use the critique skills we've honed in the business to be better at parenting. My son played little league in New York City, too. Whenever players struck out at the plate, most parents would yell out vague words of encouragement meant to boost their self-esteem: "Don't worry, you're still the best!" To me, this wasn't going to make them better hitters, and it could do a real number on their heads—how can you be the best when you just struck out? Instead, when my son struck out, my husband would say things like, "That last swing was a really good attack. But you've got to level your bat. You got way too ahead of the ball." Now that's a useful critique. The last year he played little league, he batted over .300. Such constructive comments worked off the playing field as well. Finger paintings from nursery school were never praised with broad comments such as "What a masterpiece!" I'd always go with something more specific: "I love the way you used bold strokes here, especially where the yellow contrasts with the blue. What made you put purple in the corner?" This not only encouraged a real conversation about his artwork, but it indicated that I was paying attention and had respect for his creativity.

The point here is that critique adds value to any evaluative process, from coaching little league to assessing a $40 million advertising campaign. So it's worth investing the effort into developing this skill.

And now onto. . . .

Shhhh! Blatant Cheats for a Killer Critique

Here are a few sample scenarios from creative presentations. Notice that the client comments clearly invite dialogue from the agency instead of shutting it down. They are respectful, yet probing. This is what you want. Critical (though not necessarily negative) comments that move the conversation forward are much more fruitful than dead-ended responses that tend to just elicit bone-chilling glares. The phrases below represent appropriate and constructive criticism. But they're just a sample. AdCrits are like snowflakes. Each one is unique.

Scenario One

CLIENT COMMENT: "The concept strongly communicates our strategic benefit. And I love the way that you've visualized it. The text, though, doesn't have the same power. The words communicate, but the phrasing seems a bit awkward."

AdCrit Commentary: Good isolation of elements. Good linking of elements with strategic goals. Good identification of positive. Pinpoints a negative in such a way that suggests a direction, not a solution. Much better than just saying, "I hate the headline" or "Here's how I would've written that."

AGENCY COPYWRITER RESPONSE: "Perhaps it's not what you were expecting. But let me explain what I was going for: Rather than a clever phrasing, I was hoping to capture more authentic speech. Think of it in that context and maybe the headline will work better for you."

AdCrit Commentary: Sometimes, stepping back and identifying a preconceived notion will help the client to review the work again—but with a fresh eye. Articulating the intention behind an approach also indicates a rationale, not work done on a whim. This doesn't necessarily mean it's correct, but at least it can become a point of discussion.

Scenario Two

CLIENT COMMENT: "I like the way that you've described the ads in this campaign, but could you please articulate the concept that ties them together?"

AdCrit Commentary: Nice request for pulling the ad apart in order to evaluate individual elements. Good use of the words *describe* and *articulate*. Remember: A concept is articulated; an execution is described.

AGENCY CREATIVE TEAM RESPONSE: "Absolutely. Our strategic objective is to communicate that milk is more important to us than we think. It's *so* important that you don't want to run out. Our big idea— the concept that drives the campaign—is the *absence* of milk. How do we show that? Each ad features a yummy food with a bite taken out. But no milk. This way, our readers can imagine that bite in their mouth before the 'got milk?' tagline steers readers to what's clearly missing. That's when they realize how much they want milk. They *feel* its absence. So all our ads feature those yummy foods, but—equally important—not milk. In this context, it's the absence that makes you aware of milk's importance. And wouldn't it be terrible to run out? This is what binds all the ads together. This is what drives the campaign."

AdCrit Commentary: Clear. Good repetition. Good circling back to strategy. Also: Thanks to the "got milk?" campaign (see pages 41 et seq.) for bringing this sample critique to life.

Scenario Three

CLIENT COMMENT: "A strong presentation with some excellent insights. I like so much of what you said. But I don't get all that when I look at the page. Explain to me how these ads deliver on those insights."

AdCrit Commentary: Hmmm. Sounds like the client likes what he's hearing but not what he's seeing. Not a good sign. But not an entirely bad sign, either. The comment is smartly phrased and could lead to a constructive conversation. However, there's not enough information here for the agency to respond to.

AGENCY ACCOUNT EXECUTIVE RESPONSE: "Tell us first which parts of the presentation really resonated with you. That will give us a bit more focus so we can address your concerns."

AdCrit Commentary: When the client is too vague, it's time for the agency to push back. Ask for more specifics. Don't review the entire presentation without a decent amount of client feedback first.

Scenario Four

CLIENT COMMENT [PART ONE]: "This is a dynamic layout and I personally love the design. But I'm not sure it's consistent with our brand personality."

AdCrit Commentary: Don't you love a client who can tell the difference between what's personally appealing and what's best for her brand?

AGENCY CREATIVE TEAM RESPONSE: "Well, we've pulled in a lot of existing brand elements, such as the colors and the overall tone of voice—especially in the body copy. But it's definitely more lively than before. We heard a lot of comments in the focus groups about how the last campaign looked too serious with the younger demographics we're trying to reach, which undermined some of the friendliness of the brand."

AdCrit Commentary: Nice starting point. By beginning where the client is more comfortable—existing brand colors and tone—it's easier to navigate through less familiar terrain. Also, it's always smart when the creative team references earlier research such as "the focus groups."

CLIENT COMMENT [PART TWO]: "You're right. We did agree that we needed to reach a younger audience. You've certainly accomplished this conceptually. The execution delivers on this as well. But what I'm really concerned about are some of the details in the layout. Like the type. It seems to be pushing the execution too far in this direction. It looks too youthful—more like it would appeal to teenagers."

AdCrit Commentary: Yes! The client is sticking to her ground and supporting her position with specifics. Excellent use of AdSpeak!!

AGENCY ART DIRECTOR RESPONSE: "Actually, this typeface is a little more conservative than you might think. It was used in a corporate campaign for a bank in France a few years ago. But you don't see it in the States that much. So it's still fresh here but also has some nice authority to it. I can show you some print ads from the bank campaign, if you'd like."

AdCrit Commentary: Because typography is more of a layout issue than anything else, it's smart that the Art Director responded here. Also, volunteering samples helps make comps more concrete and reveals that the Art Director's choice wasn't random but thoughtful.

CLIENT COMMENT [PART THREE]: "You've sold me. I'd love to see the other campaign, but it's not necessary. I guess I was just stuck in the typographic dark ages."

AdCrit Commentary: Backing down gracefully. If a Creative can defend his position in a way that ties it to strategic goals, the easier it is for a client to defer to his (now demonstrated) creative expertise.

Scenario Five

CLIENT COMMENT: "A brilliant campaign. The concept is both strategic and compelling: You've taken a figure of speech and given it real meaning by tying it to our product in a concrete way. This combination of familiar and fresh is very engaging. It's a strong execution as well. I like blending realism with fantasy because it's a clear outgrowth of the concept and delivers the message effectively."

AdCrit Commentary: A dream critique. Not because it's complimentary (although it will put the agency on cloud nine) but because it is so meaningfully articulated. Note that it's not just full of praise but full of substance. It identifies the strengths and repeats back the creative expression of strategic objectives. This assures the agency that even when they're not around, this client "gets it" and will be able to sell and defend this campaign up and down the line.

AGENCY RESPONSE: "Gee, thanks!"

 Visit the student study site at www.sagepub.com/tagstudy for additional online resources including web links, video clips, and recommended readings to learn more about advertising and the creative process.

Role-Playing Exercise

The best way to perfect your critique skills? Practice, practice, practice. However, this role-playing exercise shakes things up a bit and helps you develop a little empathy:

Present student work in various stages. Give everyone in the room assigned roles, such as Creative Director, Account Executive, and Brand Manager. Critique the work according to your role. Switch roles and see if your critique is different.

Bonus Exercise

Record the above critiques. Play it back and critique the critiques.

Index

About the Author

Nancy R. Tag is an Associate Professor in the Media & Communication Arts Department at The City College of New York, CUNY. She remains professionally active and has been a Creative Director at major advertising agencies in New York City, where her work has won numerous industry tributes, including two AICP award-winning TV commercials which are in the archive at the Museum of Modern Art (MoMA). Festivals in London and Chicago have also honored her work. Nancy is a graduate of the University of Pennsylvania with a Master of Arts in Media Studies from New School University.

SAGE Research Methods Online

The essential tool for researchers

Sign up now at www.sagepub.com/srmo for more information.

An expert research tool

- An **expertly designed taxonomy** with more than 1,400 unique terms for social and behavioral science research methods
- **Visual and hierarchical search tools** to help you discover material and link to related methods

- Easy-to-use navigation tools
- Content organized by complexity
- Tools for citing, printing, and downloading content with ease
- Regularly updated content and features

A wealth of essential content

- The most comprehensive picture of quantitative, qualitative, and mixed methods available today
- More than **100,000 pages of SAGE book and reference material** on research methods as well as editorially selected material from SAGE journals
- More than **600 books** available in their entirety online

Launching 2011!

$SAGE research methods online